HURRICANE I

VS

Bf 110

1940

TONY HOLMES

First published in Great Britain in 2010 by Osprey Publishing,
Midland House, West Way, Botley, Oxford, OX2 0PH, UK
44–02 23rd St, Suite 219, Long Island City, NY 11101, USA
E-mail: info@ospreypublishing.com

A CIP catalogue record for this book is available from the British Library

Print ISBN: 978 1 84603 945 4
PDF e-book ISBN: 978 1 84603 946 1

Cover artwork and battlescene by Gareth Hector
Three-views, cockpit, gunsight and armament scrap views by Jim Laurier
Page layout by Ken Vail Graphic Design, Cambridge, UK
Index by Alan Thatcher
Typeset in A Garramond
Maps and diagrams by Bounford.com
Originated by PDQ Digital Media Solutions
Printed in China through Bookbuilders

10 11 12 13 14   10 9 8 7 6 5 4 3 2 1

Hurricane I cover art

Flt Lt Ian 'Widge' Gleed downs the first of two
Bf 110Cs from III./ZG 76 to fall to his guns off
Portland Bill during the bitter fighting of 15 August
1940. The ace later recalled: 'For a second I get my
sights on another 110. He turns and gives me an easy
full-deflection shot. I thumb the trigger; a puff of
white smoke comes from his left engine. Almost lazily
he turns onto his back and starts an inverted over-the-
vertical dive. I steep-turn. Down, down he goes – a
white splash. At the same time two other splashes and
a cloud of smoke go up from the beach. Four 'planes
have hit the deck within a second.' Gleed was flying
his assigned Hurricane I (P2798)
on this occasion, and he used it to down ten German
aircraft – including six Bf 110s – between 18 May
and 30 September, 1940. (Artwork by Gareth
Hector)

Bf 110 cover art

In the same action featured in the Hurricane I cover
art, Oberleutnant Hans-Joachim Jabs of 6./ZG 76
claims the second of his three kills in his Bf 110C
during the early evening of 15 August 1940. Jabs
was credited with a Hurricane I and two Spitfires
destroyed on what the *Zerstörergeschwaders* dubbed
'Black Thursday': no fewer than 27 Bf 110s were lost
to enemy action, with ten RAF fighters downed in
return. Jabs's unit, II./ZG 76, had been escorting
60 Junkers Ju 88s from LG 1 that targeted the
British airfields at Worthy Down and Middle
Wallop; meanwhile, V.(Z)/LG 1 and III./ZG 76
helped escort 50 Ju 87s from I./StG 1 and II./StG 2
that attacked Portland naval base. Opposing the
German formations were eight Spitfire and
Hurricane I squadrons. (Artwork by Gareth Hector)

Editor's note

For ease of comparison please refer to the following
conversion table:

1 mile = 1.6km
1lb = 0.45kg
1yd = 0.9m
1ft = 0.3m
1in = 2.54cm/25.4mm
1gal = 4.5 litres
1 ton (US) = 0.9 tonnes

Author's note

Photographs for this volume were sourced from the
archives of Eddie Creek, Andy Saunders, John Weal
and the Imperial War Museum. The author would
also like to thank Bf 110 historian John Vasco for his
help with the book.

CONTENTS

INTRODUCTION

Fighter-versus-fighter combat between March and November 1940 was predominantly the domain of single-seat types such as the Spitfire I/II, Hurricane I and Bf 109E. However, flying alongside the latter during much of the action over western Europe was the twin-engined Bf 110 *Zerstörer*. The Bf 110 was designed as a 'bomber-destroyer' in the 1930s; however, during World War II its primary task was clearing a path through the enemy's defensive fighter screen for Luftwaffe bomber formations. By the spring of 1940 the propaganda surrounding the Messerschmitt Bf 110 'twin' following its successes over Poland and during the Phoney War had given the aircraft almost mythical status within the Luftwaffe. However, in the Battle of France the *Zerstörer* legend would be quickly shattered by Allied single-seat fighters.

This volume considers the Hawker Hurricane I as the Bf 110's principal opponent. The Hurricane entered service with the RAF in December 1937 as its first monoplane fighter. The Hurricane and the *Zerstörer* first traded blows during the final weeks of the Phoney War, before engaging in bloody dogfights over France as the Luftwaffe supported the Wehrmacht during the *Blitzkrieg* in the west from 10 May 1940.

The Hurricane I formed the backbone of RAF Fighter Command for the first 18 months of the war, with no fewer than 1,715 examples equipping 36 squadrons during the Battle of Britain – only half this number of units flew Spitfires. Half the weight of the Bf 110 and highly manoeuvrable, the Hurricane I also boasted a top speed of more than 300mph and sound high-altitude performance. However, the *Zerstörer* was no slouch either: it was faster than the Hurricane I in level flight in certain conditions. Nevertheless, the big, heavy bomber-destroyer was blighted by sluggish acceleration and poor manoeuvrability, which made it highly vulnerable when 'bounced' by single-seat fighters such as the Hurricane I.

It was not all doom and gloom for *Zerstörer* crews in 1940, though. The Bf 110 easily outgunned the Hurricane – and the Spitfire, for that matter. Befitting its original role as a bomber-destroyer, the Messerschmitt was armed with four 7.9mm MG 17 machine guns, with 1,000 rounds per weapon, in the nose, plus two 20mm MG FF cannon, each with 180 rounds per gun, in the lower forward fuselage. A flexibly mounted 7.9mm MG 15 machine gun was also provided for the rearward-facing navigator/radio-operator. In contrast, the Hurricane I was equipped with eight rifle-calibre 0.303-in. Browning machine guns, and these often proved to lack the destructive punch of the cannon fitted to the Bf 110 and Bf 109E.

Nevertheless, thanks to the Hurricane I's agility in combat, better tactics and eventual strength in numbers, by the early autumn of 1940 the Hawker fighter would prevail in the skies over southern England. By this time the inadequacy of the Bf 110's defensive firepower – the single rear-facing gun – and of its manoeuvrability had been cruelly exposed by RAF Fighter Command, as had the aircraft's poor acceleration and unsatisfactory top speed in combat conditions, particularly at low level. Championed by Reichsmarschall Hermann Göring before the war, the Bf 110 took a terrible beating throughout the latter half of 1940: the *Zestörergruppen* based in France and Norway lost an astonishing 223 examples during the Battle of Britain. A good number of these aircraft were claimed by Hurricane squadrons. The latter did themselves suffer losses caused by Bf 110 units, but in a far more favourable ratio of four-to-one. How the British fighter tamed the much-vaunted bomber-destroyer, and therefore helped the RAF achieve mastery of the skies over southern England, is revealed in this volume.

One in a sequence of pictures taken by legendary aviation photographer Charles E. Brown during a visit to Tangmere in early July 1940, this view shows a section of No. 601 Sqn Hurricane Is being fuelled (the aircraft to the left also appears to be having its magazines reloaded) before undertaking a convoy protection patrol off the south coast of England. The unit seems to be relying on a towable bowser rather than the usually ubiquitous Albion three-point truck. Note also the belts of 0.303-in ammunition draped over the flat-loader trolley marked '601', the solitary fire extinguisher just forward of the bowser and the fitter holding the radio access panel for the Hurricane I parked to the right of the photo.

CHRONOLOGY

1933
August
Hawker Chief Designer Sydney Camm discusses future RAF fighter requirements with Air Ministry's Directorate of Technical Development.

1934
October
Hawker design shown to Air Ministry, which in turn issues Specification F.36/34 for a monoplane fighter based on the company's project.

November
Hawker's Interceptor Monoplane now becomes the Air Ministry's F.36/34 Single-Seat Fighter – High-Speed Monoplane, powered by the Rolls-Royce PV 12. The latter is a private-venture engine that will lead directly to the Merlin.

1935
21 February
Prototype of F.36/34 Single-Seat Fighter – High Speed Monoplane ordered.

Spring
Reichsluftfahrtministerium (RLM) issues tactical requirements for a twin-engined Zerstörer ('destroyer'), and contracts to build single prototypes are given to Bayerische Flugzeugwerke AG (later renamed Messerschmitt), Focke-Wulf and Henschel.

6 November
Hurricane prototype K5083 completes is first flight at Brooklands. Three more flights follow that month.

1936
18 February
Official Hurricane trials start at Martlesham Heath.

12 May
Messerschmitt Bf 110 V1 makes its first flight, from Augsburg-Haunstetten.

3 June
British Air Ministry orders 600 aircraft from Hawker.

27 June
Air Ministry accepts the name 'Hurricane' for the new Hawker fighter.

1937
14 January
Bf 110 V2 delivered to *Erprobungsstelle* ('service trials detachment') at Rechlin for evaluation by RLM pilots. The aircraft is subsequently chosen to fulfill the *Zerstörer* role after Hermann Göring demands that production be launched without delay.

12 October
First flight of production Hurricane I.

15 December
First Hurricane Is reach the frontline, equipping No. 111 Sqn at RAF Northolt.

1938
19 April
First pre-production Bf 110B-01, powered by interim Junkers Jumo 210Ga engines, makes its maiden flight.

Early-build Hurricane Is share hangar space with Gladiator Is at RAF Kenley, Surrey, in early 1938. These aircraft all belong to No. 3 Sqn, which converted from the Gloster biplane fighter to the Hurricane I between March and July of 1938.

The original German caption to this photo says it shows 'Bf 110s of I./ZG 52 about to take off on a sortie against England'. In fact, by the start of the Battle of Britain that *Gruppe* had been redesignated II./ZG 2, although at the time this shot was taken I./ZG 52's original unit badge and fuselage codes were still being worn.

July   First production-standard Bf 110B-1s delivered to Luftwaffe.

Autumn   First examples of Bf 110B reach the front line, with I.(Z)/LG 1 of the Luftwaffe's *Lehr-Division* ('Instructional Division') receiving aircraft.

1939

January   Ten pre-production Bf 110C-0s, fitted with definitive Daimler-Benz DB 601A engines, delivered to Luftwaffe for service evaluation.

Late January   First production Bf 110C-1s issued to I.(Z)/LG 1.

Spring   Two more Luftwaffe units, I./ZG 1 and I./ZG 76, receive Bf 110C-1s.

31 August   A total of 159 Bf 110Cs delivered to Luftwaffe, with production under way at Messerschmitt, Focke-Wulf, Gothaer Waggonfabrik and MIAG.

2 September   Bf 110s form the bulk of the Luftwaffe fighter force supporting the invasion of Poland; on this date an aircraft from I./ZG 76 claims a PZL P.11c fighter, giving the *Zerstörer* its first aerial success.

3 September   Outbreak of World War II: by this time, 18 RAF squadrons equipped with Hurricane.

27 October   First Gloster-built Hurricane I makes its maiden flight.

30 October   Hurricane I of No. 1 Sqn is the first RAF aircraft to destroy a German aircraft over the Western Front in World War II.

1940

26 March   First clash between the two types, with Hurricane Is of No. 73 Sqn in combat with Bf 110Cs of 13.(Z)/LG 1.

10 May   Luftwaffe commits 319 Bf 110s in six *Geschwaders* to the invasion of France and the Low Countries.

June   By now, 386 Hurricane Is have been lost in the ill-fated defence of France, against 80 Bf 110s downed in combat.

10 July   At the start of the Battle of Britain, Fighter Command has 32 Hurricane I squadrons.

13 August   Luftwaffe commits 315 Bf 110s flown by four *Zerstörergeschwaders* to the Battle of Britain.

July–October   Fighter Command deploys 1,715 Hurricane Is in the defence of Britain, and during this period they are credited with destroying 1,593 German aircraft – four-fifths of all enemy aircraft destroyed during the Battle of Britain.

27 September   Bf 110 units suffer their worst losses in a single day during the Battle of Britain, when 19 aircraft are shot down during raids on southern England.

1 October   III./ZG 26 downs two No. 607 Sqn Hurricane Is – the last Hawker fighters to be credited to the Bf 110 during 1940.

31 October   Between 10 July and this date, 223 Bf 110s have been downed.

17 November   The last *Zerstörer* to be credited to the Hurricane I in 1940 after No. 17 Sqn claims four Bf 110s from I./Erpr.Gr. 210 destroyed.

DESIGN AND DEVELOPMENT

HURRICANE

The unsung hero of the Battle of Britain, the Hurricane could trace its lineage back to 1912 and the establishment of the Sopwith Aviation Company by leading pioneer aviator Thomas Sopwith. The firm soon established an enviable reputation for itself through the production of aeroplanes such as the Tabloid, Pup, Camel, Dolphin and Snipe. However, Sopwith was badly affected by the massive reduction in defence spending immediately following World War I, and the company was forced into liquidation.

Determined to start again, Thomas Sopwith re-formed the company under the name of H. G. Hawker Engineering in recognition of the work done by his Australian chief test pilot Harry Hawker during World War I. Hawker was killed practising for the Hendon Air Display in July 1921. In 1923 Sydney Camm joined Hawker as a senior draughtsman. During a relationship spanning 43 years, Camm would work on 52 different aircraft types with production totalling 26,000 airframes. In 1925 Camm replaced George Carter as Hawker's chief designer; after this time Camm concentrated on creating military aircraft for the RAF. Undoubtedly his most famous products during the interwar period were the stunningly beautiful Hart two-seat bomber and Fury single-seat fighter, both of which were powered by the Rolls-Royce Kestrel inline engine.

In early 1933 Camm began looking at the feasibility of producing a monoplane fighter. He believed the biplane formula adhered to by the RAF since World War I was deadlocked, and he hoped to break that deadlock. Nevertheless, despite discussions with the Air Ministry's Directorate of Technical Development at this time he failed to secure official support for his proposal. Regardless, Hawker's board backed its chief designer, giving him approval to press on with the aircraft – dubbed the 'Fury Monoplane' – as a private venture. This did present Camm with some problems, as Hawker designer Dr Percy Walker recalled:

> As a private venture, the design from the beginning was subject to certain limitations, mainly owing to the need to control costs. The firm was compelled to apply existing design techniques to their monoplane, and make use of existing machine tools and workshop methods. This meant a structure composed mainly of steel tubes covered with fabric. The use of fabric for wing-covering produced a problem which was far from easy to resolve. By the standards of the time, the speed of the Hurricane was very high indeed, much faster than any of its biplane predecessors. Never before had fabric wing-covering been subject to such speeds and loading for any length of time.

Work on the Fury Monoplane started in earnest in the spring of 1933, with Camm and his team initially producing a design that essentially paired a Fury fuselage with a single low wing of 38ft span. The aircraft, fitted with a fixed, spatted undercarriage, was powered by a 660hp Rolls-Royce Goshawk engine. It was estimated that this engine would give the fighter a top speed of 280mph. By comparison, the Fury I biplane could achieve 207mph in level flight.

In early 1934 Rolls-Royce announced that it was developing a 12-cylinder, liquid-cooled engine, designated the PV 12. The power-to-weight ratio of this powerplant was significantly better than that of the Goshawk engine, and Rolls-Royce believed the PV 12 would produce at least 1,000hp. Camm quickly realised that the PV 12 had to be incorporated into his monoplane fighter. This move meant significant changes to the design were necessary, to the point where the new aircraft's link to the Fury became tenuous. Accordingly, the new aircraft was renamed the 'Hawker Interceptor Monoplane'.

In October 1934 Air Ministry officials examined the Hawker design. They were so impressed with what they saw that they in turn issued Specification F.36/34 for a monoplane fighter based on the company's project. The next month Hawker's Interceptor Monoplane, powered by the Rolls-Royce PV 12, became the Air Ministry's 'F.36/34 Single-Seat Fighter – High Speed Monoplane'. The PV 12 would eventually mature into the mighty Merlin.

On 21 February 1935 the Air Ministry placed an order with Hawker detailing the creation of the first prototype of the F.36/34 Single-Seat Fighter – High Speed Monoplane. Although when building the new monoplane fighter Hawker's designers were tempted to embrace such cutting-edge techniques as stressed-skin construction, the designers realised that the need to rapidly mass-produce the aircraft would mean they would have to

No. 1 Sqn Fury IIs cruise along in Aircraft Close Vic, Sections Close Vic formation for the benefit of the visiting *Flight* photographer in autumn 1938. At this time the unit was in the process of converting to the Hurricane I at RAF Tangmere, Sussex. Before the war, Fighter Command squadrons spent much of their time practising this kind of formation flying rather than focusing on modern fighter tactics and aerial gunnery.

OPPOSITE
This aircraft, part of the first
production batch of 500
aircraft built by Gloster
Aircraft Company at its
Brockworth plant in
Gloucestershire, was
delivered new to No. 56 Sqn
in early 1940. Passed on
to No. 601 Sqn in May,
it was regularly flown by
Plt Off J. C. U. B. McGrath from
RAF Tangmere during the
early phase of the Battle of
Britain. Indeed, McGrath
claimed ten victories with this
aircraft between 11 July and
13 August, including three
Bf 110s. However, P2690
was one of two No. 601 Sqn
Hurricane Is lost on the latter
date over Portland Bill, fellow
ace Plt Off H. C. Mayers being
forced to take to his
parachute over Weymouth
Bay after his aircraft was hit
by fire from a Bf 110 of
I./ZG 2. Mayers had claimed a
Zerstörer probably destroyed
moments earlier.

rely on methods that had served them well since World War I. More modern construction techniques would have required creating new jigs and tools for use on the factory floor, as well as retraining the Hawker workforce. Consequently, the Single-Seat Fighter – High Speed Monoplane design was constructed using established concepts, modified to suit the requirements of the more modern aircraft.

For example, the steel-tube longerons that provided the main support for the fuselage were surrounded by a secondary structure of wooden formers and stringers that was in turn covered with fabric along the length of the fuselage from the tail to the cockpit. From the cockpit forward the fuselage was covered with light metal panels. The fighter's ailerons were fabric-covered, but its split-edge trailing flaps boasted duralumin covering. The PV 12 – soon to be named the Merlin – was mounted on steel tubes. Initially, this state-of-the-art engine was used to drive a simple wooden two-bladed Watts propeller, as fitted to the biplane Fury I. As with most monoplane fighter designs of this period, the Hawker aircraft featured a retractable undercarriage. Crucially, this retracted inwards, giving the undercarriage a wider stance when extended and making the fighter better suited to operations from rough fields.

By October 1935 the prototype, bearing the serial number K5083, was nearing completion at Hawker's Kingston plant. In due course the airframe was delivered by road to the company's assembly shed at nearby Brooklands, and at month's end the complete aeroplane was rolled out. On 6 November Hawker's chief test pilot, Flt Lt P. W. S. 'George' Bulman, took K5083 on its maiden flight from Brooklands. Three more flights quickly followed. Fellow Hawker test pilot Philip Lucas made one of these early hops, later commenting: 'We found the aeroplane easy to fly, stable in flight and on the ground, and with a much better view than anything we had flown before.'

Following three months of company flight trials, during which the aeroplane attained a speed of 325mph at 16,500ft, in February 1936 prototype K5083 was transferred to the Aeroplane and Armament Experimental Establishment (A&AEE) at Martlesham Heath for evaluation by RAF test pilots. The report issued at the end of these trials noted among other things that the aeroplane had a service ceiling of 35,400ft. It also confirmed that K5083 was the world's first fighter capable of exceeding 300mph in level flight.

In the wake of the favourable A&AEE report, Hawker's management became aware

The Hurricane fighter
and Henley dive-bomber
prototypes await their next
flights at Brooklands (note
the banked racing track in he
background) in the summer
of 1937. The Henley was also
powered by a Merlin I engine
and featured Hurricane I
outer wing panels. Just 200 of
the type would be built and
used for target towing.

HURRICANE I

31ft 5in.

13ft 0in.

40ft 0in..

P2690

of rumours that the Air Ministry was likely to recommend that the company's design be put into volume production. Bert Tagg, a member of Hawker's production staff from 1935, recalled:

> The Hawker directors demonstrated their confidence in the aeroplane by agreeing in March 1936 that production should be initiated ahead of contract, with a policy to plan tooling and facilities for 1,000 aeroplanes. This early board decision gave a lead of considerable importance in the light of subsequent events.

Historians have since argued that committing the aircraft to production at such an early stage in its development had the effect of disallowing further improvements to the design that could have given the fighter a level of performance comparable with that of its future adversary, the Bf 109E. However, it is estimated that if the Hawker fighter had indeed been delayed so as to allow for future development – a fate which initially befell the Spitfire – then during the Battle of Britain 600 fewer examples would have been delivered to the RAF. This in turn would have almost certainly allowed the Luftwaffe to achieve aerial supremacy on the Western Front, arguably facilitating the invasion of Britain.

On 3 June 1936 the Air Ministry issued a contract to Hawker to build 600 examples of the F.36/34 Single-Seat Fighter – High Speed Monoplane; later that same month the design was officially named the 'Hurricane'. In July K5083 provided the public debut for the new Hawker fighter when it participated in the Hendon Air Display.

Hawker's Kingston and Brooklands facilities would not be able to cope with production on the scale requested by the Air Ministry. Fortunately, however, in 1934 the company had acquired the Gloster Aircraft Company, and this was charged with volume Hurricane production from 1938. That same year, Hawker's brand-new Langley plant also began delivering Hurricanes, which was just as well considering that the company received a follow-on contract for 1,000 aeroplanes in November 1938.

By this time the problems K5083 had experienced with the Merlin I powerplant had been well and truly cured. This was also just as well, for the issues of reliability regarding the Rolls-Royce engine had been so concerning that both Hawker and the Air Ministry had decided to wait for the improved 1,030hp Merlin II before commencing production of the Hurricane I. The first example of the Hurricane I, L1547, made its maiden flight on 12 October 1937. This machine differed from K5083 not only in having the more powerful Merlin II, but it also had a revised and strengthened canopy, ejector exhaust stubs, and revised undercarriage doors.

L1548 became the first Hurricane I to be issued to Fighter Command when on 15 December 1937 it was delivered to No. 111 Sqn at RAF Northolt, which had previously been equipped with Gloster Gauntlet I/II biplane fighters. The unit was fully equipped by early 1938. Like the prototype, the first Hurricane Is in service had two-bladed fixed-pitch Watts wooden propellers, but these were subsequently replaced by de Havilland two-position three-bladed propellers and, finally, de Havilland or Rotol constant-speed units. However, aircraft equipped with Watts propellers did see combat in France in May–June 1940; the final examples were not replaced until after Dunkirk.

Another feature of early-production Hurricane Is was fabric-covered wings. This caused some problems for No. 111 Sqn in its early days with the fighter. Unit pilot and future 1940 ace Plt Off Roy Dutton recalled that 'at high speed the wing gun panels sometimes partially blew out and the wing fabric distended like sausages between the ribs'. By 1939 stressed-skin metal wings were being manufactured, and these were considerably lighter, stronger and stiffer in terms of both bending and torsion. Heating units for the guns were also fitted within the wings themselves: at the time of the Munich Crisis in September 1938 it had been revealed that Hurricane pilots were unable to fire their weapons at heights above 15,000ft due to the guns' mechanisms being frozen.

By the time Germany invaded Poland on the morning of 1 September 1939, some 497 Hurricane Is had been delivered to 18 squadrons within RAF Fighter Command.

Pilots had found the new machine a joy to fly, as 19-year-old future ace Plt Off Roland Beamont of No. 87 Sqn remembered:

To a newcomer, the Hurricane was an immensely powerful but not very demanding aeroplane. Its wide-track undercarriage, stable and responsive flying characteristics and reliable engine and hydraulic system resulted in a general atmosphere of confidence on the squadron, so that the newcomer had no reason to become apprehensive.

Hurricane Is of No. 79 Sqn, based at RAF Biggin Hill, Kent, fly over the North Downs at medium altitude in Aircraft Close Line Abreast formation for press photographers aloft in an RAF Anson. This particular shot was taken on 8 August 1939 during one of the last RAF peacetime Air Defence Exercises by a *Kent Messenger* photographer. Exactly 12 months later fighter pilots would be repeating the self-same routine several times a day, although now they would be intercepting real Luftwaffe aircraft in their hundreds, rather than a handful of Blenheim Is hastily repainted with white crosses.

The young men of Fighter Command, confident in the ability of their Hurricanes to take the fight to Germany, would find themselves embroiled in a bitter struggle for aerial supremacy initially over western France and then over southern England for much of 1940. Proving that both they and their aircraft were more than up to this task, Hurricane pilots would emerge at year's end with four-fifths of the aerial kills credited to the RAF in 1940.

From 1941 the Spitfire began to dominate the ranks of Fighter Command. Nevertheless, the Hurricane remained in production until September 1944, by which time 12,780 examples had been built in the UK and 1,451 under licence in Canada. The aircraft's appearance and performance altered remarkably little over seven years, yet the soundness of Sydney Camm's original design had allowed the Hurricane to remain a viable weapon of war right through to VJ-Day.

Bf 110

As this book will demonstrate, the Bf 110 was thoroughly unsuited to dogfighting with the Hurricane, which it was called upon to do during the spring and summer of 1940. For a fighter to be successful in aerial combat, speed, acceleration and manoeuvrability were all required. The Bf 110 possessed the first of these, but sorely

Ranking *Zerstörer* ace Oberleutnant Hans-Joachim Jabs flew several Bf 110Cs marked 'M8+NP' during 1940. All wore ZG 76's fearsome 'shark's mouth' on the nose, and this particular aircraft, seen here in the markings worn in June 1940, bore six kill symbols on its fin to denote Jabs's successes during the Battle of France. The ultimate fate of this aircraft is unknown.

Four Bf 110s pictured at Messerschmitt's Augsburg plant in spring, 1938. The third aircraft in line is the Bf 110 V4 prototype; it wears the German civil registration D-AISY. The remaining three aircraft are factory-fresh Bf 110Bs without armament. The V4 has been painted in the light colour scheme synonymous with prototype machines of this period. All aircraft also carry the pre-war red tailfin bands with a swastika in a white circle. The three Bf 110Bs were subsequently transferred to a s*chwere Jagdgruppe* in Barth, on the Baltic coast, during the summer, while the V4 was sent to the Rechlin test centre.

lacked the latter two. In its defence, the aircraft was never designed for a dogfighting role. Bayerische Flugzeugwerke AG (BFW) had created the Bf 110 as a long-range strategic *Zerstörer* whose primary job was to clear a path through the enemy's defensive fighter screen for Luftwaffe bomber formations. Such a concept was not new: in World War I the most successful aircraft of this type had been the British Bristol F2 Fighter flown by the Royal Flying Corps and the RAF.

However, interwar fighter designers generally stuck with what they knew: single-seat biplanes with a high power-to-weight ratio and modest wing-loading. In the early 1930s the *status quo* was shattered. The monoplane revolution was made possible by the advent of monocoque fuselages, cantilever tail units, retractable undercarriages and stressed-skin single- or double-spar wings. The new breed of interceptors, like the biplane fighters before them, were still only modestly armed and equipped with barely adequate fuel tankage so as not to erode their speed and manoeuvrability. Limited range was the order of the day. However, now air forces were demanding fighters with combat endurance that could accompany bombers on missions deep into enemy territory. The technology available to designers in the 1930s did not allow the production of a single-engined machine that could perform this role, hence the resurrection of the concept of the twin-engine strategic fighter. According to pre-eminent Luftwaffe historian William Green:

> In essence, the strategic fighter was envisaged as a warplane embodying high performance and heavy armament, coupled with sufficient endurance to permit the escort of bombers, deep-penetration offensive sorties over enemy territory and the maintenance of standing patrols at substantial distances from its base. Time was to prove that no entirely successful strategic fighter would emerge from the considerable effort devoted to the evolution of this category of warplane in the years preceding World War II.

Few less enviable tasks could have faced the combat aircraft designer of the 1930s than that of evolving a satisfactory strategic fighter. Such a warplane had, of necessity, to be a compromise, and compromises are rarely good enough. Conflicting requirements were inherent in the concept, and one could only be fulfilled at the expense of another. The strategic fighter had to possess a performance higher than, or at least comparable with that of the more specialised defensive fighters by which it was likely to find itself opposed, and if it was to succeed in fending off determined attacks on the bomber formations, which one of its primary tasks was to protect, manoeuvrability was a prime requisite. Yet firepower, the fuel necessary to attain the desired range and suitability for a multiplicity of auxiliary roles dreamed up by planning staff, dictated a relatively large aircraft of twin-engined configuration. In consequence, some sacrifice of manoeuvrability had to be accepted.

Bf 110C

39ft 8.5in.

13ft 6.5in.

53ft 4.75in.

M8 NP

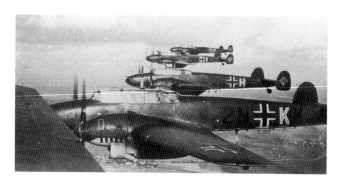

On the outbreak of war, two of the three *Zerstörergruppen* with Bf 110s still had Jumo-powered B-models on strength. Here, *Berta*s of 2./ZG 1 are flying escort for a *Stukagruppe en route* to Warsaw on 8 September 1939.

The strategic fighter requirement formulated in Germany in 1934 called for the creation of a *Kampfzerstörer* – a multi-role aircraft whose primary mission was as a long-range fighter sweeping ahead of bomber formations. Many senior figures within the Luftwaffe's Technical Department opposed the concept on the grounds that the resulting aircraft would be too large and heavy, and therefore slow and unwieldy, to perform any one task effectively. However, the Luftwaffe's commander-in-chief Hermann Göring was convinced that Germany needed a long-range fighter, and a directive was duly given to the effect that development of the *Kampfzerstörer* should proceed with great haste.

The specification called for a twin-engine all-metal three-seat monoplane armed with flexibly mounted cannon and featuring an internal bomb-bay. Seven aircraft manufacturers received the specification; they included BFW, which had just started work on the Bf 109 prototypes. *Diplomingenieur* ('academically qualified engineer') Willy Messerschmitt and his chief engineer, Walter Rethel, also felt that the *Kampfzerstörer* would be a failure if designed according to the official specification, so they chose to ignore many of the requirements and focused instead on ultimate performance. The proposals submitted by Focke-Wulf and Henschel followed the specifications more closely, however, and they received three-prototype contracts from the *Reichsluftfahrtministerium* (RLM). BFW appeared to have missed out, but influential World War I ace Ernst Udet, who was a close friend of Messerschmitt, brought pressure to bear on the RLM. Consequently, the company also received a contract to build three examples of its aircraft, now designated the Bf 110.

Concerns over the viability of the *Kampfzerstörer* finally resulted in an alteration to the RLM requirement in the spring of 1935, so that a dedicated *Schnellbomber* ('high-speed bomber') was now specified. The demand for a *Zerstörer* remained, however, the aircraft now being exclusively a 'bomber-destroyer'. The proposed Bf 110 fighter was well placed to fill the latter role, since its lean, sleek design allowed an impressive top speed.

Following static tests and taxiing trials at Augsburg-Haunstetten, the prototype Bf 110 V1 performed its first flight – with Rudolf Opitz at the controls – on 12 May 1936. The poor reliability of the twin Daimler-Benz 600A engines hampered flight testing, but BFW pilots were able to report that the fighter had a marginal stability problem at low to medium speeds, but essentially good handling at higher speeds. Also noted was the Bf 110's weak acceleration and poor manoeuvrability, although its top speed of 314mph in level flight did somewhat offset these drawbacks. A tendency to swing violently during take-off and landing was also reported. In fact, the aircraft would suffer from poor ground handling throughout its long career.

Ongoing engine problems meant that the second prototype, Bf 110 V2, did not fly until 24 October 1936. This aircraft was subsequently delivered to the *Erprobungsstelle* at Rechlin on 14 January 1937 for evaluation by RLM pilots. Unsurprisingly, the

Bf 110 outperformed both its rivals, the Fw 57 and Hs 124, in the *Zerstörer* role, as the latter aircraft had been built more as *Kampfzerstörer* than bomber-destroyers. Upon hearing this news, Göring demanded that BFW commence production without delay – the long-range heavy fighter had started to figure most prominently in the Luftwaffe's advanced war planning.

The first production model, the Bf 110A, was to have been powered by the 986hp DB 600Aa. However, persistent problems with this powerplant led to its abandonment in favour of the uprated DB 601, and cancellation of the Bf 110A. The new engine also suffered a troublesome gestation period, resulting in Messerschmitt being forced to switch to the interim 680hp Junkers Jumo 210Ga engine for its production-series Bf 110B. The first of ten pre-production Bf 110B-1s flew on 19 April 1938, and production-standard machines slowly began to reach I.(Z)/LG 1 of the Luftwaffe's *Lehr-Division* in the autumn. The latter unit was responsible for formulating tactics and techniques for the projected *schwere Jagdgruppen* ('heavy fighter groups', redesignated *Zerstörergruppen* on 1 January 1939).

The first *Gruppe* to be equipped with the Bf 110C, in late January 1939, was operational trials unit I.(Z)/LG 1 based at Barth. There already appears to be a problem with the port DB 601 engine of 2. *Staffel* aircraft 'L1+A12' in the foreground.

Only 45 Bf 110Bs were built, as this version's performance was deemed inadequate for combat tasks thanks to its Jumo 210Ga engines. These aircraft did nevertheless play an important role because they let crews evaluate equipment and armament and develop operational techniques.

By late 1938 the problems with the 1,100hp DB 601A-1 had at last been ironed out, allowing Messerschmitt to start production of the definitive Bf 110C-1 model. This variant differed from the B-model not only in having new engines, but also in the deletion of the deep radiator bath beneath each engine and the addition of a shallow glycol radiator outboard of the powerplant on the underside of each wing. Small oil coolers were also incorporated into the lower portion of the engine nacelles.

The Bf 110 production programme was now running way behind schedule, but from late 1938 it was given the highest priority. Ten pre-production Bf 110C-0s were delivered to the Luftwaffe in January 1939 for service evaluation, and by month's end the first production Bf 110C-1s had reached I.(Z)/LG 1. Deliveries to I./ZG 1 and I./ZG 76 also began during the spring and early summer. By 31 August 1939 the Luftwaffe had received 159 Bf 110Cs, with ongoing production under way at Messerschmitt, Focke-Wulf, Gothaer Waggonfabrik and MIAG. The Bf 110s in service were flown by hand-picked crews mainly drawn from Bf 109-equipped units; all this gave the *Zerstörergruppen* elite status. The aircraft they used was shrouded in an aura of invincibility generated by the German propaganda machine. Keen to prove the worth of his 'Ironsides' – so named after Oliver Cromwell's Parliamentary cavalry of the 17th century – Göring reportedly ordered the Luftwaffe to throw its entire force of *Zerstörer* (just 90 serviceable aircraft) into the assault on Poland. Would the Bf 110 live up to its elite billing?

TECHNICAL SPECIFICATIONS

HURRICANE I

HURRICANE I (EARLY-BUILD)

Early-build Hurricane I L1732 was issued to No. 43 Sqn on 6 December 1938 and damaged while being flown by Flt Lt Caesar Hull on 29 August 1939, when he hit an airfield obstruction at RAF Tangmere. On 18 September 1939 the aircraft was sent for repair to the Morris Works at Cowley (Oxford), where this picture was taken. From No. 43 Sqn, L1732 went on to serve with Nos. 7 and 6 Operational Training Units and finally with No. 286 Sqn. The fighter was written off on 14 May 1943, while serving with the latter unit, after it hit high-tension cables and crashed at Torcross, Devon. Clearly in 1939 nobody had heard of health and safety in the workplace, judging by the precarious jacking and trestling methods employed here.

The first 600 Hurricane Is delivered to the RAF differed very little from the solitary prototype, K5083. Although the latter had initially been flown without armament, eight-gun wings were fitted to the aircraft in the summer of 1936 and the prototype made its first flight in this configuration on 17 August that year. As mentioned, the first production-standard Hurricane I, L1547, was fitted with the more powerful and more reliable 1,030hp Merlin II engine in place of K5083's 1,025hp Merlin C.

As well as the change in powerplant, the production aircraft had a revised canopy with internal strengthening, a bulletproof windscreen (added in early 1939), simplified undercarriage doors, an aerial mast, an enlarged rudder including a trim tab and formation light on the trailing edge, landing lights in the wing leading edge and 'kidney' exhaust stubs. The latter were in turn replaced from mid-1938 by 'ejector' exhaust stubs after Rolls-Royce discovered that by fitting these, the Hurricane I's maximum speed could be boosted by 5mph. The ejector stubs vented gases to the rear instead of at right-angles to the slipstream, as had previously been the case with the 'kidney stubs'.

Standing up in his cockpit, Sgt T. B. G. 'Titch' Pyne of No. 73 Sqn keeps a weather eye on the two armourers loading a belt of 0.303-in ammunition into the starboard wing magazine of his aircraft, at Étain-Rouvres, France, in late 1939. Pyne would lose his life in combat with Bf 110s from III./ZG 26 north of Vouziers on 14 May 1940.

The first 60 Hurricane Is also lacked the small strake beneath the rear fuselage that later became standard for all examples built from February 1938 – none of the first three units to re-equip with the Hawker fighter initially received modified Hurricane Is. The strake's addition was found to aid high-speed spin recovery.

As built, early Hurricane Is had a length of 31ft 5in. and a wingspan of exactly 40ft. The entire forward quarter of the fuselage was taken up by the engine compartment, containing the Merlin II. Immediately behind this was an armour-plated firewall, then the reserve fuel tank (with 28 Imperial gallons) and the cockpit, with bulletproof windscreen and sliding canopy (the latter was subsequently made jettisonable). Two 33gal self-sealing fuel tanks were installed in the wing roots on either side of the fuselage centre section, while the eight 0.303-in Browning machine guns were housed in either wing in closely grouped banks of four each, outboard of the undercarriage and sited so as to let them fire outside of the propeller arc. With most equipment and systems grouped around the aircraft's central fuselage and forward quarter, the fabric-covered steel-tube-and-longeron rear fuselage was virtually empty. Its sole purpose was to carry the tail section.

Production of the first batch of Hurricane Is – 600 aircraft – ran from October 1937 to October 1939. These machines were issued to Nos. 111, 56, 87, 85, 73, 32, 1, 43, 79 and 151 Sqns in 1938, and Nos. 213, 46, 501, 504 and 605 Sqns up to 3 September 1939. By the end of September the first examples from a follow-on order for 300 Hurricane Is had started to roll off the Hawker production line at Kingston.

HURRICANE I (LATE-BUILD)

By the start of the Battle of Britain in July 1940, Fighter Command units were receiving definitive late-build Hurricane Is as attrition replacements for aircraft written off in combat or flying accidents. Many of the upgrades seen on these machines were also fitted to early-build Hurricane Is at RAF maintenance units (MUs) and civilian-run repair depots when aircraft required overhaul or battle-damage rectification.

One of the first and most obvious changes to be made was the replacement of the big Watts wooden two-blade, fixed-pitch propeller with a three-blade metal or

Veteran late-build Hurricane I P3886 of No. 601 Sqn being serviced on the perimeter dispersal at Exeter Airport in mid-September 1940. Note the aircraft's natural-metal cowling over its reduction gear, which had been fitted in the wake of an engine failure suffered by the fighter on 26 July. Once repaired, this aircraft enjoyed success while being flown by No. 601 Sqn aces Sgt L. N. Guy (a Ju 88 shared on August 15) and Flg Off C. R. Davis (a shared Ju 87 and a shared Bf 109E on 18 August, followed by a Bf 110 probable on 31 August). By the time this photograph of the aircraft was taken, both pilots had been killed in action.

composite unit. The Watts propeller had been in widespread use within the RAF since the mid-1920s, and it had been adequate for frontline types as long as speeds – particularly in the dive – did not exceed 360mph. Above that speed the 'aircraft drove the propeller'; tip speeds would near compressibility (the speed of sound) and the propeller would overspeed in relatively coarse pitch, potentially causing serious damage to the engine. The Watts propeller's blade pitch angle had been selected as a compromise between requirements for take-off (when a fine pitch is most efficient) and combat (when coarse settings were optimal).

The solution to these problems was a variable-pitch propeller: one that could have its blade angles changed in flight by the pilot. The first successful design was produced by US company Hamilton Standard in the early 1930s. A three-blade metal propeller of 11ft diameter that allowed two pitch settings – 30.5 degrees fine and 42.5 degrees coarse – was trialled on Hurricane I L1562 on 29 August 1938. However, although this was an improvement on the Watts, it was far from ideal: the fighter's take-off run was greatly reduced, but its performance at altitude was little better than when fitted with the wooden propeller. The Hamilton Standard propeller also failed to cure the problem with overspeeding in a dive. Finally, being bracket-operated, the propeller (built under licence by de Havilland) routinely sprayed oil onto the windscreen in flight.

Fortunately, by late 1938 the British company Rotol had designed a usable constant-speed propeller. This was 10ft 6in. in diameter and had a pitch range of 23 to 53 degrees. It was operated by the pilot via a pitch-control lever located in the cockpit alongside the throttle. The pilot could now vary the pitch of the propeller and select the best possible blade angle according to the fighter's speed and power requirements. The Rotol propeller was controlled using a hydraulic constant-speed unit (CSU), which prevented engine overspeeding in high-speed dives. According to leading Hurricane historian Frank Mason, 'As well as improving the Hurricane I's rate of climb, the Rotol propeller enabled the aeroplane to fly for endurance more efficiently and was regarded by many as one of the decisive factors contributing to the Hurricane's brilliant combat success during the Battle of Britain.'

The Hamilton Standard/de Havilland propeller was bracket-operated, so there was no requirement for hydraulic powerlines running from the central fuselage to the hub via the shaft. This meant the propeller could be fitted to the Merlin II without modification. However, the Rotol propeller relied on hydraulic power to change the blade pitch, which did require powerlines to the hub. It also had a self-contained CSU mounted at the front of the engine itself. In order to accommodate these changes Rolls-Royce produced the modified Merlin III, which had a 'universal' propeller shaft catering for all current and future types of propeller.

Hawker began trials with the Merlin III and the Rotol propeller in late January 1939, and from the second batch of Hurricane Is onward either this combination or the Merlin III plus the de Havilland two-pitch propeller was fitted as standard. From late 1939, earlier-built aircraft were also modified, although Watts-equipped machines remained in the frontline into the early summer of 1940.

The other major structural change for the Hurricane I during this period was the introduction of stressed-metal wings. Use of such wings had been considered by Hawker right from the start, but the Air Ministry had been keen to get the aircraft into service as quickly as possible. This in turn meant that virtually all the 600 aircraft in the first production run and the first 80 in the second batch of 300 were completed with fabric-covered wings.

By late 1938 Hawker designers were busy working on the all-metal Tornado and Typhoon fighters intended as replacements for the Hurricane. The company was keen to gain experience with stressed-skin construction techniques by introducing all-metal Hurricane wings, but the Air Ministry was anxious not to slow the flow of fighters so as to allow their introduction. Nevertheless, Hawker test-flew a set of metal wings on 28 April 1939, after which it fabricated a production-type jig to allow these to be built *en masse*. Having reviewed the flight performance data for the metal-wing Hurricane I, the Air Ministry agreed that the company should start production straight away. However, these wings were initially to be fitted to damaged aircraft returned to Hawker for repair. Stocks of new wings were then supplied to MUs so that fighters in storage awaiting delivery to operational squadrons could also be modified. An individual wing change took little more than three hours to complete, yet there were still many fabric-wing Hurricane Is in the frontline in 1940 (the last one having been assembled at Brooklands in March), despite there being large stocks of metal wings at Kingston, Brooklands, Hucclecote and various MUs.

Additional armour plating was also fitted to late-build Hurricane Is. Initially, the aircraft boasted just a single piece of plating forward of the cockpit, but with the advent of the cannon-armed Bf 109D a bulletproof windscreen was installed (despite objections by cost-conscious Air Ministry officials). Following No. 1 Sqn's early experiences in combat during the 'Phoney War', which led to the unit fitting steel plating from a wrecked Battle to one of its Hurricane Is in the field, additional armour plating was inserted aft of the pilot's seat as standard equipment to all RAF fighters. Both these vital modifications had been added to all production machines by the spring of 1940.

Finally, the original TR 9B radio was replaced by the improved TR 9D in 1939, the former having been found lacking both in range and audible clarity. This change required the introduction of a new aerial mast and lead in place of the original 'pole' type.

Most of these changes began to appear on new-production Hurricane Is constructed by both Hawker and Gloster from late October 1939. By then the combined output from Hawker's Kingston and Brooklands plants, as well as the Gloster site at Brockworth, was five new late-build Hurricane Is per day. One of the pilots to be issued with such an

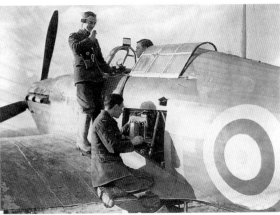

RAF pilots were plagued by poor radio communication throughout 1940, as the pre-war TR 9B equipment proved anything but reliable, and the TR 9D replacement was little better. Here, radio fitters (note the 'electrical' flash sewn onto the right sleeve of their tunics) from No. 601 Sqn tinker with the set fitted in Hurricane I P3886 at RAF Tangmere.

HURRICANE I GUNS

The Hurricane I boasted four Browning 0.303-in machine guns in each wing. Re-arming a Hurricane I usually took a two-man team 30 minutes. Each Browning was loaded with 332 rounds of ammunition which, at 20 rounds per second, would last just 17 seconds. The magazines were grouped together in a single bay in each wing and accessible from above, allowing them to be replenished more quickly than those of the Spitfire. Although the Brownings were very reliable, they were regularly criticised by RAF pilots for not providing enough punch when it came to shooting down German fighters and bombers.

aircraft was future ace Plt Off Tom Neil of No. 249 Sqn, who described the Hurricane I in detail in his book *Gun Button to 'Fire'*:

My first Hurricane was brand-new, its number P3616 and shortly to bear the code 'GN–F'. It had a constant-speed Rotol propeller, which was quite new to me. Also, it was tight and bouncy, like a new car, with the intriguing smell of fresh paint. Very impressive. I was delighted.

The Hurricane was little more than an updated version of the old Hawker Hart and Fury, with only one wing, of course. The family likeness was immediately evident, the cockpit being much the same with the pilot sitting in space and lots of darkness below and behind him. There were many more instruments, naturally, but after my brief experience with the Spitfire I the layout seemed bitty and the cockpit generally less well finished. The throttle I especially disliked; after the Spit, a flimsy little lever – very insignificant!

The pilot sat a good deal higher in a Hurricane than in a Spitfire and, through a hood that could be opened in stages, saw rather more of what was going on. Also, there was a feeling of solidity about the aeroplane, the wings especially being much thicker and the wheels widely spaced so that it sat on the ground very firmly and in a no-nonsense way. Happily, too, the radiator was centrally placed so it caught the slipstream when taxiing, and there was not the eternal business of counting the seconds before the engine boiled as with the Spitfire.

In the air, the pilot immediately detected a feeling of steadiness. The ailerons were lighter than those of a Spit, markedly so at speed, but the elevator was much less sensitive. The Hurricane couldn't be bent with one finger – with two hands, even – but having said that, there was no feeling of heaviness, the controls, if anything, being better balanced than those of the Spitfire.

If I was expecting the aircraft to be noticeably slower than the Spit, I was to be pleasantly surprised. There was not much in it at the lower end of the speed range so that we still flew around at about 230mph. However, the Hurricane just did not have the legs of a Spit or its sprightly acceleration in a dive; moreover, at its best climbing speed of 140mph, though it went up more steeply, it did so at a much slower speed. *And* – very disappointingly – there was no rudder bias, which meant that on a full-throttle climb, the aircraft required a heavy right boot on the rudder and an even heavier left one when descending quickly. A thoughtless and irritating omission, I always thought.

On the whole though, we were not disappointed. Whilst it may not have had the refinements of a Spit, our recent acquisition was rock-solid and possessed an obvious ruggedness and strength. No shrinking violet, this! Furthermore, its reputation as a fighter was as impressive as its unbending toughness.

Plt Off Neil's P3616, then flown by Plt Off M. A. King, was subsequently shot down by a Bf 110 over Southampton at 1355hrs on 16 August 1940. King was killed when his parachute collapsed.

Bf 110

Although a handful of Bf 110Bs participated in the invasion of Poland from 1 September 1939, by the time the RAF started to encounter the *Zerstörergruppen* in late March 1940 all units had been equipped with Bf 110Cs. A small number of D-models also saw action during the Battle of Britain.

Bf 110C

This version of the Bf 110 was hastily put into mass production in late 1938 following the resolution of the powerplant problem that had plagued the *Zerstörer* for more than a year. The construction of the Bf 110 remained the same from the prototype through the various operational variants, with some 6,170 examples being built by war's end.

A rare colour view of two Bf 110Cs from II./ZG 1 on patrol over the Baltic Sea in the early spring of 1940. Note the *Gruppe*'s unusual 'three-wasps-above-cloud' emblem on the noses of both machines, the closest of which also features a single victory bar on its port tailfin. Both aircraft also have their propeller spinner tips painted in *Staffel* colours – a standard unit identification marking throughout the *Zerstörer* force in the early war years.

This photo-reconnaissance Bf 110C-5 of 4.(F)/14 was shot down by Hurricane Is from Red Section of No. 238 Sqn on 21 July 1940, the aircraft crash-landing virtually intact in a cabbage field at Home Farm near Goodwood, Sussex. It was quickly restored to airworthiness by the RAF using parts taken from a Bf 110C from 9./ZG 76 that had been shot down by Hurricane Is ten days earlier. The aircraft was then extensively flown in a series of comparative tests against Spitfires and Hurricane Is. Note the clear-view panel behind the MG FF cannon ports for the Rb 50/30 camera to shoot through.

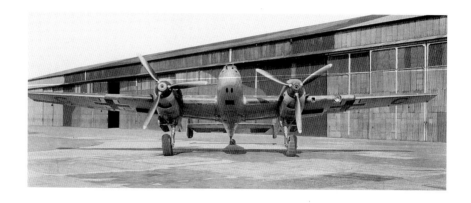

Following the structural formula so successfully adopted for the Bf 109, Messerschmitt built the Bf 110's wing in halves. Each half was attached to the fuselage at the leading edge and at the top and bottom main spar booms. The wing structure itself consisted of a single spar at 39 per cent chord, lateral stringers spaced 12in. apart and former ribs at intervals of 10in. The wing was then covered with stressed-metal skinning. Handley-Page automatic slots occupied 40 per cent of the outboard leading edge, while the entire wing trailing edge was fitted with hydraulically operated slotted flaps and ailerons with external mass balances.

The oval-section all-metal stressed-skin fuselage structure housed up to three crewmen, with the pilot seated over the wing leading edge, the radio operator/navigator immediately aft of him and the rear gunner over the wing trailing edge. In frontline service, a single crewman usually performed both the radio-operator/navigator and gunner's roles in order to save weight. All cockpits were enclosed by a single large, transparent canopy. The aircraft's tail assembly was of cantilever monoplane type, fitted with endplate fins and rudders. Both the main undercarriage and tailwheel retracted aft, with the former housed in the engine nacelles. The two Daimler-Benz DB 601 engines, driving three-bladed variable-pitch propellers, were carried by cantilever mountings attached directly to the wing spar, and fuel was housed in four tanks, split two on either side of the fuselage fore and aft of the wing spar.

Hurricane I and Bf 110C-4 comparison specifications

	Hurricane I	Bf 110C-4
Powerplant	1,130hp Merlin III	2 × 1,100hp DB 601A-1
Dimensions		
Span	40ft 0in.	53ft 4.75in.
Length	31ft 5in.	39ft 8.5in.
Height	13ft 0in.	13ft 6.5in.
Wing area	258 sq ft	413 sq ft
Weights		
Empty	4,982lb	9,920lb
Loaded	7,490lb	15,300lb
Performance		
Max speed	328mph at 20,000ft	349mph at 22,960ft
Range	505 miles	530 miles
Rate of climb to 20,000ft	8.1 min	10.2 min
Service ceiling	34,200ft	32,000ft
Armament	8 × 0.303-in. Brownings	5 × 7.92mm MG 17 2 × 20mm MG FF

A head-on view of a Bf 110C-6 fitted with 30mm MK 101 *Kanonen* in place of the standard 20mm MG FF weapons. Just 12 examples of this 'up-gunned' variant were built, and as this photograph shows, the lower forward fuselage had to be heavily modified in order to accommodate the weapon. The aircraft made its combat debut in the spring of 1940, with 1./ZG 1 during the Battle of France.

Like the Bf 110B before it, the C-model was armed with four 7.9mm MG 17 machine guns in the upper nose and two 20mm MG FF cannon in a weapons pack in the underside of the fuselage immediately beneath the radio operator/navigator's position. The latter crewman could change the MG FF's ammunition drums in flight as necessary. He also had a rearward facing 7.9mm MG 15 machine gun on a flexible mounting in the rear cockpit.

Aside from the crucial engine change, the Bf 110C also featured more angular wingtips which resulted in a slight decrease in the fighter's wingspan and wing area.

By the end of 1939, some 315 Bf 110C-1s had been built, allowing three *Zerstörergruppen* to be fully equipped with the aircraft. Production output surged from 26.25 Bf 110C-1s a month in 1939 to 102.6 throughout 1940; this in turn meant a rapid expansion of the *Zerstörer* component within the Luftwaffe.

In early 1940 the C-2 variant also began to reach the frontline, this version featuring an improved high-frequency Lorenz FuG 10 radio in place of the original FuG IIIaU. This change also prompted an overhaul of the central cockpit area occupied by the radio operator/navigator. A handful of Bf 110C-3s appeared in the spring of 1940, these aircraft being airframes that had been retrofitted with the improved MG FF/M cannon. This let Messerschmitt remove the external breech fairing that protruded from the underside of the Bf 110. The C-4 was essentially a Bf 110C-2 with the improved MG FF/M fitted in place of the initial MG FF. This variant also introduced nominal armour protection for both the pilot and gunner.

The photo-reconnaissance optimised Bf 110C-5 entered service with the *Aufklärungsstaffeln* in the early summer of 1940. This variant was externally identical to the C-4, but had the twin MG FFs replaced by an Rb 50/30 camera mounted above an aperture in the cockpit floor. The later C-5/N variant featured improved 1,200hp DB 601N engines.

The MG FF cannon were also replaced in the Bf 110C-6, but this time by a single 30mm MG 101 weapon. Substantial reworking of the lower central forward fuselage was required to allow the *Kanone* to fit, and in the end only 12 aircraft were built

The enormous size of the Bf 110D's ventral fuel tank is well illustrated in this frontal view. The picture shows how drastically the Bf 110's otherwise relatively clean lines were altered by the ventral fairing. It is hardly surprising that combat reports penned by RAF pilots who met these monstrosities on 15 August 1940 described them as 'Dornier bombers'! The aircraft, from the Norway-based I./ZG 76, were engaged by Fighter Command when 21 of them were escorting bombers from *Luftlotte* 5, sent to attack targets in northeastern England. Seven Bf 110Ds were lost, a number of them being claimed by Hurricane I pilots from Nos. 79, 605 and 607 Sqns. In the wake of this disastrous foray across the North Sea, I./ZG 76 played no further part in the Battle of Britain.

(utilising modified C-5 fuselages). The first examples of this variant were delivered to I./ZG 1 in the spring of 1940, and at least one was shot down while serving with I./Erpr. Gr. 210 during the Battle of Britain.

The final Bf 110C variant was the C-7 fighter-bomber, which was fitted with two ETC 500 racks beneath the fuselage that allowed the aircraft to carry a pair of 500kg bombs. Powered by DB 601N engines, the Bf 110C-7 also boasted a strengthened undercarriage to allow it to cope with the increased bombload.

The C-series was finally phased out of production in the spring of 1941.

Bf 110D

The main external difference between the Bf 110C- and D-models was the extended rear fuselage of the latter variant. This housed a dinghy and emergency supplies. The D-0 was initially conceived as a fighter with increased range, this being facilitated by fitting a large *Dackelbauch* ('dachshund-belly') fairing under the centre fuselage. Made of plywood and covered in fabric, this housed a fuel tank with 1,050 litres and an oil tank

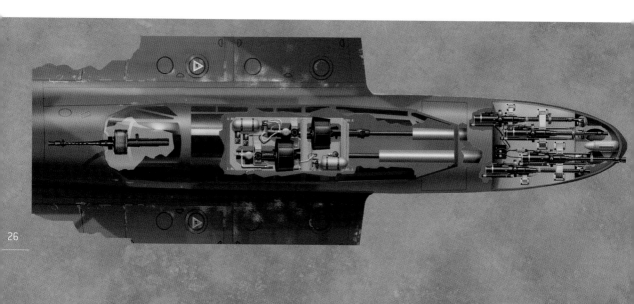

with 106 litres. This variant was issued primarily to I./ZG 76 in Norway in the spring of 1940, and saw limited action with the unit during the Battle of Britain.

The Bf 110D-0/B was the first dedicated fighter-bomber variant of the *Zerstörer* to reach the frontline. Fuselage bomb racks had first been trialled by Messerschmitt in April 1940, and after the modification was evaluated at the Rechlin test centre the company was ordered to produce a version of the D-model fitted with ETC 250 bomb racks housed in a rectangular fairing mounted on the centreline fuselage immediately beneath the cockpit. The *Dackelbauch* fairing was omitted. The first examples were issued to the newly formed I./Erpr. Gr. 210 in July 1940.

The Bf 110D-1 was a stillborn reconnaissance version of the D series, while the limited-run D-2 had two ETC 1000 racks fitted to allow it to carry a pair of SD 1,000kg bombs. The aircraft was also plumbed for wing-mounted auxiliary fuel tanks.

Oberleutnant Victor Mölders, brother of well-known ace Werner Mölders, flew numerous versions of the Bf 110, and he related his feelings about the aeroplane to Belgian historian Armand van Ishoven in 1979 for inclusion in the latter's book *Messerschmitt Bf 110 At War*:

> The Bf 110 felt as if it had been tailored for me. It was faster than any bomber, could stay in the air double the time of the Bf 109, and with the help of the wireless operator, one could approach one's target unseen in the clouds. It was heavily armed with its four machine guns and two cannon, and even if the wireless operator could do little harm with his sole machine gun, a rearward-firing observer gave a pilot a comfortable feeling.
>
> Of course, there were drawbacks to the Bf 110 – one could not fly it like a Bf 109. The manoeuvrability and climbing speed of the Bf 110 compared badly with the Bf 109. Most enemy fighters were also better suited to dogfighting – something proved beyond doubt during the Battle of Britain.

This Bf 110D-0 of 1./Erpr. Gr. 210, carrying two SC 500 bombs on ETC 500 racks housed within a rectangular fairing, is believed to be the aircraft flown by the unit's acting *Gruppenkommandeur*, Oberleutnant Werner Weymann, on 5 October 1940 when he and his *Bordfunker*, Unteroffizier Erwin Hübner, were shot down into the Channel and killed. Although only operating relatively few Bf 110s, Erpr. Gr. 210 achieved some stunning successes – and suffered heavy losses – with the aircraft during the Battle of Britain.

Bf 110C GUNS

The licence-built 20mm Oerlikon MG FF *Kanonen* were mounted in a weapons pack that was directly installed into the underside of the Bf 110, beneath the radio operator's position; it was this airman's duty to replace the ammunition drums in flight once they were empty. Each drum contained 180 rounds. The MG FFs were mounted to fire slightly upwards, and were also staggered. The upper nose of the aircraft housed four 7.92mm Rheinmetall MG 17 machine guns, and it could also be fitted with an ESK 2000a gun-camera. The weapons, their ammunition feed apparatus and the gun-camera could be accessed by the groundcrew via a single removable cowling. The four MG 17s were set in place in a staggered configuration, which allowed the ammunition feed and spent cartridge chutes to sit completely enclosed in the upper nose cowling. Each weapon had its own dedicated ammunition box holding 1,000 rounds per gun.

THE STRATEGIC SITUATION

The Bf 110 was heavily involved in the opening act of World War II, reportedly on the direct instructions of Hermann Göring himself. Keen to see his bomber-destroyers blooded in combat, Göring committed all 90 of the Luftwaffe's serviceable *Zerstörer* to the invasion of Poland, which began shortly before dawn on 1 September 1939. The aircraft were split evenly between I.(Z)/LG 1, I./ZG 1 and I./ZG 76, the *Zerstörergruppen* in turn being deployed at almost equidistant intervals along Germany's common border with Poland. Each unit was positioned so as to be able to lend maximal direct support to one of the three main axes of Wehrmacht advance.

Providing fighter escort for Heinkel He 111 and Dornier Do 17 bombers, as well as Junkers Ju 87 dive-bombers of the 1. and 2. *Fliegerdivisionen* and the *Luftwaffe-Lehrdivision*, the Bf 110 *Gruppen* were the principal fighter units involved in the campaign. The shorter-ranged Bf 109 *Geschwaders* were in the main held back for home defence purposes: it was feared that French and British bombers would attack German cities upon those countries' declaration of war in support of Poland on 3 September.

The *Zerstörergruppen* claimed their final aerial victories of the Polish campaign on 15 September, by which time the Bf 110 had indeed lived up to its pre-war billing. Crews were credited with more than 40 aerial victories while flying independent patrols deep into enemy territory or providing bomber escort, and the aircraft was also used effectively in the ground-attack role in support of the advancing Wehrmacht. Admittedly, the Bf 110's main adversaries were obsolescent Polish PZL P.11c fighters; however, the PZLs' nimbleness came as an unpleasant surprise to the Luftwaffe and resulted in a number of *Zerstörer* being lost in return. Ground fire also inflicted some casualties.

The end of the Polish campaign was followed by an eight-month period known as the *Sitzkrieg* or 'Phoney War', as it was dubbed by the Allies. Aircraft from both sides would periodically venture across the respective defensive borders (the Maginot Line in France and the *Westwall* or Siegfried Line in Germany) on tentative reconnaissance flights. Most action during this period took place over the *Dreiländereck* (Three-Nations' Corner) on the northernmost section of the Franco-German border, as this was the shortest route for Allied reconnaissance aircraft heading for the Ruhr.

A scoreboard in the making, applied ahead of I.(Z)/LG 1's 'wolf's-head' emblem. Although the first victory bar is marked '1.9.39', none of the others is dated. Since no I.(Z)/LG 1 pilot achieved five kills in Poland, this would suggest either that one of these claims was later disallowed or that the photograph was taken at a later date, on the Western Front.

The Luftwaffe used this relatively quiet period for reinforcement and rapid expansion as it sought to boost its strength along the Rhine. All three *Zerstörergruppen* that had been committed to the invasion of Poland were quickly transferred to bases in western Germany, and although no new units were activated the opportunity was taken to re-equip the seven original *Gruppen* still flying the Bf 109 with Bf 110s.

The RAF also made the most of the 'Phoney War' to prepare itself for the inevitable onslaught. Following Britain's declaration of war on 3 September 1939, a long-standing agreement between Britain and France was invoked that saw the former rapidly despatch British Army and RAF units to the Continent. From an RAF standpoint, this British Expeditionary Force (BEF) comprised two distinct elements. The first of these was the Advanced Air Striking Force (AASF), made up of Fairey Battle III medium bombers from Bomber Command's No. 1 Group and, eventually, Blenheim IVs from No. 2 Group. These units were mainly tasked with strategic bombing operations, and initially had no dedicated cover from Fighter Command – the French *Armée de l'Air* was responsible for protecting AASF assets.

The second element, which was to operate closely with BEF ground forces, comprised the whole of No. 22 (Army Co-operation) Group, plus a quartet of

'No. 79 Sqn, scramble!' Although staged for the press corps at RAF Biggin Hill on 8 August 1939, this shot nevertheless captures the atmosphere of the final peacetime Air Defence Exercises.

In May 1940, Bf 110 *Zerstörer* units were mainly based along Germany's northwestern border with France and Belgium. From here they could range deep into the Low Countries in support of Luftwaffe bomber units charged with knocking out Allied airfields and other key military installations as part of the *Blitzkrieg* in the West. As the Wehrmacht captured vast swathes of Allied territory the units would relocate to airfields in France.

■	Bf 110 Units in the West, May 1940	
1.	Niedermendig	I./ZG 26
2.	Krefeld	III./ZG 26
3.	Kirchhellen	I./ZG 1
4.	Gelsenkirchen-Buer	II./ZG 1
5.	Darmstadt-Griesheim	I./ZG 2
6.	Cologne-Wahn	II./ZG 76
7.	Kaarst/Neuss	II./ZG 26
8.	Neuhausen ob Eck	I./ZG 52
9.	Mannheim-Sandhofen	V.(Z)/LG 1

Hurricane I squadrons and two Blenheim I units formerly of No. 1 Group. Emphasising the air elements' designated close-support role, the bulk of No. 22 Group squadrons were equipped with Lysander IIs. The four Hurricane I units sent to France were Nos. 1, 73, 85 and 87 Sqns, and upon arrival between 9 and 15 September these became part of No. 60 (Fighter) Wing.

Flying from airfields in eastern France near the borders with Belgium and Germany, aircraft from these units would be the first British fighters to encounter the Bf 110 during the latter stages of the Phoney War. By then both the Hurricane I and the *Zerstörer* had seen sporadic action against unescorted bombers sent to probe either sides' defences. Undoubtedly the most spectacular of these inevitably one-sided clashes came on 18 December 1939, when I./ZG 76 attacked 22 RAF Wellingtons sent to attack targets in the port of Wilhelmshaven. In what was later referred to as the 'Battle of the German Bight', 11 bombers were destroyed and six more so badly damaged that they subsequently crashed or crash-landed.

The first clash between RAF Hurricane Is and Luftwaffe Bf 110s came shortly after noon on 26 March 1940, when three aircraft from No. 73 Sqn engaged 16 *Zerstörer* from V.(Z)/LG 1 that were escorting a solitary Do 17P over the Franco-German border. Honours were shared, as a single aircraft from both sides was damaged in an inconclusive engagement. This action perfectly summed up Phoney War operations, with German reconnaissance and bomber aircraft and their fighter escorts probing Allied territory in restricted numbers, and British and French aircraft doing much the same thing in return. However, larger formations of German fighters began to appear as the weather improved in the early spring of 1940, as Flg Off Paul Richey of No. 1 Sqn recalled in his book, *Fighter Pilot*:

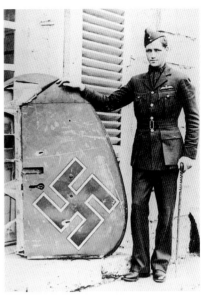

German fighters had previously shown reluctance to cross the frontier or to engage our fighters. They had evidently maintained a standing patrol on their own side, only crossing to our side in small numbers and always very high. But now the German fighters came across in big formations: sometimes three squadrons of 109s would do a sweep as far as Metz and Nancy. The 110s had made their first appearance at the end of March, in close squadron formation and very high, only engaging when pressed into it by our Hurricanes. It was obvious that the Germans were practising offensive tactics, and it looked as though the bust-up might come soon.

Flg Off Paul Richey claimed eight and one shared victory during the *Blitzkrieg*, four of these against Bf 110s. He was also shot down twice by *Zerstörer*, on 11 and 15 May, before being badly wounded four days later after despatching three He 111s in a matter of minutes. Richey is seen here following a spell in the American Hospital in Paris, posing with the fin of a Bf 110 at Châteaudun on 14 June 1940. He presented this 'trophy' to No. 1 Sqn following the unit's epic engagement with I./ZG 26 on 11 May. In Richey's left hand is his 'shooting' stick, with nine notches carved into it to denote his victories.

Richey's reading of the situation was correct. On 10 May 1940 Germany's armed forces launched the invasion of France and the Low Countries. In a forerunner of what was to come in the Battle of Britain, practically the whole of the Luftwaffe's *Zerstörer* strength was brought together for the *Blitzkrieg* in the west. In all, nine *Zerstörergruppen* flew missions from airfields scattered along the *Westwall*, these units being split between *Luftflotten* 2 and 3. More than 350 Bf 110C/Ds and upwards of 800 aircrew prepared themselves to gain control of the skies over western Europe.

The campaign itself had two components, code-named Operation *Yellow* and Operation *Red*. Operation *Yellow* would begin with an all-out attack on Holland and Belgium which, it was calculated, would cause the BEF and French northern armies to rush to the aid of the Low Countries. With the Allies out of their prepared defensive positions along the Maginot Line, the Wehrmacht would launch its primary offensive in the vulnerable rear of the Allied forces, with the main Panzer force sweeping around behind them and racing for the Channel. The Low Countries and Anglo-French divisions would be cut off from supplies and reinforcements, and quickly defeated. Operation *Red* would then swing into action, with German troops advancing west across the Somme into central France.

During the opening round of the *Blitzkrieg* the Bf 110 units would be called upon to repeat the tactics they had employed so effectively in Poland. On the southern and central sectors of the new front, the bulk of the *Zerstörergruppen* flew long-range escort

missions aimed at crippling enemy airpower, exactly as had been done in September 1939. In France alone the Luftwaffe struck nearly 50 Allied airfields. Taken by surprise, the defenders offered scant resistance to the marauding German formations. Over Belgium too, where bombers were escorted by II. and III./ZG 26 during attacks on Charleroi and Antwerp, few Allied aircraft were seen.

Simultaneously, to the north over Holland, ZG 1 was carrying out ground-attack sorties to soften up Dutch airfield defences prior to paratroop and glider landings. During these sweeps I./ZG 1 claimed 26 aircraft destroyed on the ground. Those aircraft that did manage to get into the air in a bid to oppose the German bomber formations were quickly dealt with by the Bf 109Es and Bf 110s of the *Jagd-* and *Zerstörergruppen* (I. and III./ZG 26 and I. and II./ZG 1) assigned to *Luftflotte* 2. On 12 May, with the launching of the armoured thrust at the rear of the stretched Allied forces, *Luftflotte* 3's units (II./ZG 26, II./ZG 76, I./ZG 52 and V.(Z)/LG 1) at last joined in the action too.

Reacting quickly to the German invasion, the British government ordered the Commander-in-Chief of Fighter Command, Air Chief Marshal Sir Hugh Dowding, to send three more Hurricane units (Nos. 3, 79 and 501 Sqns) to France immediately. Dowding had fought Whitehall politicians throughout the Phoney War to stop more of his precious squadrons being dispatched to France, despite repeated requests from the French government since September 1939. Some 452 Hurricane Is had been committed to the Battle of France by 21 June.

Aside from the units permanently based in France (more arrived as the battle progressed), Hurricane I squadrons based in southeast England also started to send large formations of aircraft on patrols across the Channel. They would often refuel at airfields in France in mid-mission, continue with their patrol and then return to their bases in the UK.

Hurricane I units were quickly told to target German bombers rather than provide fighter escorts for the Battles and Blenheims of the AASF. The Hurricanes proved to be very successful in the bomber-destroyer role, but this deployment also meant that Hurricane I units routinely ran into the Luftwaffe's own dedicated bomber-destroyer, the Bf 110, as this was heavily tasked with escorting Do 17s, He 111s and Ju 88s. Indeed, despite the Bf 109E being the numerically dominant German fighter throughout the *Blitzkrieg*, the Bf 110 encountered the Hurricane I far more frequently. The types fought each other on a near-daily basis from

A *Kette* of II./ZG 76 'Sharksmouths' revel in their mastery of the French skies as Allied forces are pushed back towards the Channel coast in late May 1940.

Parked in No. 1 Sqn's muddy dispersal area on the edge of Vassincourt airfield, Hurricane I N2358 is being refuelled from the unit's Albion three-point bowser while its fitter tinkers with the engine. This aircraft was coded 'Z' by the squadron soon after arrival at Vassincourt in November 1939, and following brief service with No. 43 Sqn at Acklington it retained this marking when it was passed on to No. 73 Sqn at Rouvres in early 1940. N2358 was one of 12 Hurricane Is hastily plucked out of the frontline or from maintenance units and sent to Gloucester for refurbishment before being shipped to Finland in late February 1940 to serve with the Finnish Air Force.

10 May through to the start of the Dunkirk evacuation (Operation *Dynamo*) on 26 May, and although the *Zerstörergruppen* did on occasion inflict heavy losses on the Hurricane units, this was usually achieved through sheer weight of numbers. As the Polish P.11cs had shown eight months earlier, in a one-versus-one dogfight a single-engined fighter like a Hurricane I could easily out-turn a cumbersome Bf 110, and as the latter rarely used the hit-and-run tactics favoured by Bf 109E units, the *Zerstörergruppen* suffered particularly heavy losses.

Nevertheless, by the end of May the BEF was in the throes of evacuation back to England from Dunkirk, and much of northern France was in German hands. Bf 110 units had moved forward into occupied territory to keep pace with the advancing ground forces, leaving them ideally placed to participate in the bitter aerial battles that took place over the evacuation beaches along the Channel coast in late May and early June. The completion of *Dynamo* at midnight on 2–3 June signalled the end of the first part of the campaign in the west. It had cost the *Zerstörergruppen* more than 60 Bf 110s destroyed.

On 21 June came the effective end of the RAF's operations in France, when the very last battle-weary fighters of No. 501 Sqn departed the Channel Islands for Croydon. Just 66 Hurricanes returned to Britain following the BEF's withdrawal. Fighting in France continued as part of Operation *Red* until a ceasefire was agreed on 25 June.

Paris was declared an open city following the Franco-German Armistice of 25 June 1940, and it made an ideal backdrop for this propaganda shot showing a *Schwarm* of V.(Z)/LG 1 machines over the Arc de Triomphe (bottom left). A wartime censor has tried to doctor this photograph, but has only partially obliterated the individual aircraft letters. The *Gruppe* badge and otherwise full unit codes are still clearly visible.

By then a number of the Bf 110 units that had played such a key part in the success in the West had returned to Germany to rest, recuperate and refit in preparation for an all-out attack on Great Britain, while others settled into their new bases in northern France and made good their losses.

UNIT ORGANISATION

As with the *Blitzkrieg* in the West, *Luftflottenkommando* 2 and 3 would again be at the forefront of the fighting during the Battle of Britain, controlling most of the Bf 110 units assigned to the offensive through the offices of *Jagdfliegerführer* 2 and 3 and VIII. *Fliegerkorps*. The odd unit out was I./ZG 76, assigned to *Luftflottenkommando* 5 in Stavanger, Norway.

Unlike British fighter squadrons at the time, which only officially formed into wings as the RAF went on the offensive in 1941, German fighter and *Zerstörer* units had been grouped together since before the war. The *Jadgwaffe* equivalent to a typical 12- to 16-aircraft squadron in Fighter Command in 1940 was the *Staffel*, which consisted of nine aircraft (rising to as many as 16 as the war progressed). A *Staffel* was led by a *Staffelkapitän* of Oberleutnant or Hauptmann rank, who in turn controlled a further 20 or more aircrew and 100 or more groundcrew. *Staffeln* were usually numbered 1, 2, 3 and so on.

In 1940, typically, three *Staffeln* and the *Stab* (headquarters flight) would be assigned to a single *Gruppe*, which was the Luftwaffe's basic flying unit for operational and administrative purposes. Normally, one complete *Gruppe* occupied a single airfield, and this was usually the case during the Battle of Britain, with linked *Staffeln* being spread among austere sites in the Pas-de-Calais, Normandy and Brittany. The *Gruppenkommandeur* was usually a Hauptmann or Major, and he led between 35 and 40 pilots and more than 300 groundcrew. *Gruppen* were usually numbered I., II., III. and so on.

The *Geschwader* was the largest Luftwaffe flying unit to have a fixed strength of aircraft. Two complete *Zerstörergeschwaders* flew Bf 110s during the Battle of Britain, but only ZG 26 had all of its aircraft based in France. Assigned to *Luftflottenkommando* 2 in the Pas-de-Calais, it operated alongside *Stab*, II. and III./ZG 76, with I./ZG 76 being based in Norway. *Luftflottenkommando* 3 in Normandy and Brittany controlled *Stab*, I. and II./ZG 2 (there was no III. *Gruppe*), as well as V.(Z)/LG 1. Additionally, Bf 110C/D fighter-bombers were flown by Erpr. Gr. 210 within *Luftflottenkommando* 2.

Assigned some 90–95 aircraft when fully equipped, a *Geschwader* was usually led by a *Kommodore* of Major, Oberstleutnant or Oberst rank. The *Zerstörergeschwaders* were in turn locally controlled by *Jagdfliegerführer* (those involved in the Battle of Britain were also numbered 2 and 3), which issued operational directives to the frontline flying units. The *Jagdfliegerführer* were in turn part of the larger, locally based *Fliegerkorps*, which were ultimately subordinated to the *Luftflotten* (of which the Luftwaffe had four in 1940). These were self-contained organisations, each with its own fighter, bomber, reconnaissance, ground-attack and transport units.

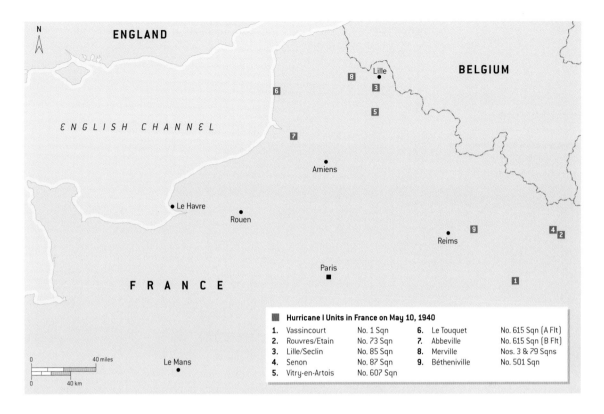

Hurricane I Units in France on May 10, 1940		
1. Vassincourt	No. 1 Sqn	6. Le Touquet	No. 615 Sqn (A Flt)
2. Rouvres/Etain	No. 73 Sqn	7. Abbeville	No. 615 Sqn (B Flt)
3. Lille/Seclin	No. 85 Sqn	8. Merville	Nos. 3 & 79 Sqns
4. Senon	No. 87 Sqn	9. Bétheniville	No. 501 Sqn
5. Vitry-en-Artois	No. 607 Sqn		

The *Zerstörergruppen* slowly began to return to the Channel coast in strength during July and early August 1940, with some 315 Bf 110s in France by 13 August. Opposing them were 29 squadrons of Hurricanes, totalling 462 aircraft. As mentioned, the RAF units were not organised into air fleets or groups as per the Luftwaffe model. Instead, all fighters in Great Britain were centrally controlled by Fighter Command, headed by Air Marshal Dowding.

All three *Gruppen* of ZG 26 were heavily involved in fighting over southern England during the Battle of Britain. Here, Hauptmann Ralph von Rettberg, *Gruppenkommandeur* of II./ZG 26, briefs his assembled crews for the next mission. The unit's 'clog' emblem is prominently displayed on the pennant that was always 'flown' outside *Gruppe* HQ, in this instance at Lille.

Fighter Command had been formed in 1936, as one of four commands, when the flying strength of the RAF was broken up by the Air Ministry, mainly in response to German rearmament. With its HQ at Bentley Priory, Fighter Command initially controlled three groups created by Dowding to defend Great Britain: No. 11 Group was charged with protecting the Southeast, No. 12 Group the Midlands and No. 13 Group the North and Scotland. On 8 July 1940, following the fall of France, No. 10 Group was established to cover potential German targets in the Southwest.

Each Group was split up into Sectors which were given letters for identification purposes, although ultimately they would be known by the name of their sector station – the airfield controlling them. Defending London and the Southeast, No. 11 Group would be the vital organisation in Britain's defence in 1940. Its HQ was at Uxbridge, not far from Bentley Priory, and its sectors (centred on London) were lettered A, B, C, D, E, F and Z, controlled from Tangmere, Kenley, Biggin Hill, Hornchurch, North Weald, Debden and Northolt, respectively.

Hurricane I units based at these stations, and nearby smaller satellite airfields, constituted the 'teeth' of Fighter Command in 1940. Typically, each squadron would have up to 16 aircraft, with a similar number of pilots, usually split up into two flights, labelled 'A' and 'B'. Each flight was led by a flight commander of flight lieutenant rank and in overall command was a squadron leader. Large airfields such as Biggin Hill or Kenley would be home to three or four fighter units, while smaller satellite fields could only handle a single squadron.

This picture of an armourer from 5./ZG 26 may have been staged for the photographer's benefit, as the ammunition for the MG 17s was carried in a box in the lower nose and fed up to the gun breech.

During the summer of 1940 Hurricane I pilots relied on other assets within the command to effectively take the fight to the Luftwaffe. Undoubtedly the most important of these was the chain of radar stations built during the late 1930s along the south and east coasts of England and in Scotland. Codenamed Chain Home (CH), the stations – there were 18 between Portsmouth and Aberdeen – were able to detect and track enemy aircraft approaching from medium or high level at distances of more than 100 miles. The equipment proved unable to track aircraft flying at altitudes below 5,000ft, however, so in late 1939 the RAF introduced Chain Home Low (CHL) stations that could detect aircraft flying at 2,000ft some 35 miles from the British coastline. CHL sites were interspersed between CH towers.

A complex network of landlines linking these various sites with Fighter Command HQ and group and sector operations rooms was another asset that proved vital during the Battle of Britain. When enemy aircraft were detected by radar, their grid position, altitude and estimated strength were passed via landline to the Filter Centre at Fighter Command HQ. Once the plot had been classified 'hostile', it was passed to the Operations Room and noted as a marker on the situation map. This information was also relayed to relevant fighter groups and sector operations rooms, appearing on their situation maps also. The fighter controller at the group HQ tasked with defending the area that appeared to be threatened by the 'hostile' plot then ordered his units to 'scramble'. It was crucial that this order was given early enough to allow the fighters to get up to the raiders' altitude.

Radar of this period could not track aircraft overland, so once German formations crossed the British coastline the Observer Corps would take over responsibility for tracking them. The observers would pass plot information via a landline to their own group HQ, which in turn relayed details to Fighter Command's Filter Centre for onward transmission.

Once airborne, a fighter unit remained under the radio control of one of the Sector operations rooms, the fighter controller guiding the squadron until its pilots visually sighted the enemy. At this point the formation leader would call 'Tally ho!' over the radio, signalling to the controller that he needed no further help from him. By the summer of 1940 Fighter Command squadrons were thoroughly familiar with ground-based fighter control operations, having regularly exercised with this system before the war. According to noted Battle of Britain historian Dr Alfred Price, 'in the forthcoming air actions over Britain, the ground control system would be Fighter Command's ace of trumps'.

BATTLE OF BRITAIN

For the second and last time in the wartime Luftwaffe's history, the Battle of Britain would see virtually the entire frontline strength of Bf 110s concentrated in one area – along the Channel coast. Once again, these aircraft would be charged with achieving aerial supremacy as the German *Kampf-* and *Stukageschwaders* strove to knock out Fighter Command in preparation for the seaborne invasion of southern England, codenamed Operation *Seelöwe* ('*Sealion*').

Historians have split the Battle of Britain into four phases, commencing in early July with the *Kanalkampf*. During this period, German aircraft attempted to deny the English Channel to British shipping by attacking coastal convoys and port facilities on England's south coast. To this end, a special mixed-force battlegroup of Do 17s and Ju 87s was set up, complete with its own dedicated Bf 109E escort. Although no *Zerstörergruppe* was

Exhibiting a vast array of flying clothing, No. 242 Sqn pilots pose in front of Sqn Ldr Douglas Bader's Hurricane I (note the squadron leader's pennant beneath the cockpit) at RAF Coltishall, Norfolk, in late September 1940. The men are, from left, Plt Off D. Crowley-Milling (four and one shared destroyed, two probables and one and one shared damaged), Flg Off H. N. Tamblyn (five and one shared destroyed, one probable and two damaged; killed on 3 April 1941), Flg Off P. S. Turner (ten and one shared destroyed, three unconfirmed destroyed, one probable and eight damaged), on the wing, Sgt J. E. Savill (one destroyed), Plt Off N. N. Campbell (one and two shared destroyed; killed 17 October 1940), Plt Off W. L. McKnight (17 and two shared destroyed and three unconfirmed destroyed; killed on 12 January 1941), Sqn Ldr D. R. S. Bader (20 and four shared destroyed, six and one shared probables and 11 damaged), Flg Off G. E. Ball (six and one shared destroyed and three damaged), Plt Off M. G. Homer (one damaged; killed on 27 September 1940); and Plt Off M. K. Brown (killed on 21 February 1941). Tamblyn, Bader and McKnight claimed 13 Bf 110s destroyed between them in 1940.

Eight *Zestörergruppen* occupied a series of sites in northwestern France during June and July 1940 in preparation for Operation *Seelöwe* ('Sealion'). Units based in the Normandy region primarily encountered RAF fighter units from No. 10 Group, while those in the Pas de Calais were routinely opposed by Spitfires and Hurricane Is from Nos. 11 and 12 Groups.

Bf 110 *Zerstörer* Units, August 1940

1.	Yvrench-St Omer	I./ZG 26
2.	Crécy-St Omer	II./ZG 26
3.	Barly-Arques	III./ZG 26
4.	Abbeville-Yvrench	II./ZG 76
5.	Laval	III./ZG 76
6.	Caen	V.(Z)/LG 1
7.	Caen-Carpiquet	I./ZG 2
8.	Guyancourt	II./ZG 2

attached to this command, Bf 110 operations were often flown in conjunction with and in support of its activities. The *Zerstörer* thus spent the last three weeks of July 1940 over the Channel and England's south-coast harbour towns.

The *Kanalkampf* would last until 12 August, and although Fighter Command succeeded in matching the Luftwaffe in trying circumstances, it suffered significant losses – including 48 Hurricane Is destroyed and many more damaged. A number of these aircraft had been claimed by Bf 110s conducting *freie Jagd* ('free-hunt') sweeps independently of the bombers, seeking out RAF fighters; other RAF losses had occurred when the *Zerstörergruppen* were called on to defend bomber formations. The Bf 110 units had also suffered heavy losses during this period, with 34 aircraft downed. Most fell victim to Hurricane Is including some of the 16 Bf 110s destroyed on 11 and 12 August during large-scale raids on the naval base at Portland, Dorset.

Gloster-built Hurricane I R4218 served with No. 601 Sqn from 15 August to 7 October 1940, when it was written off in a forced landing following combat over Portland Bill. During this period the aircraft was used mainly by Australian-born ace Plt Off Howard Mayers, who used it to claim two Do 17s destroyed and one damaged on 31 August, a Do 17 destroyed and a half-share in a probable Bf 110 on 4 September and a Bf 110 destroyed and a Do 17 damaged on 25 September. Mayers was at the controls of R4218 when it was hit in the glycol tank by return fire from a bomber while engaging German raiders targeting the Westland aircraft factory at Yeovil on the afternoon of 7 October.

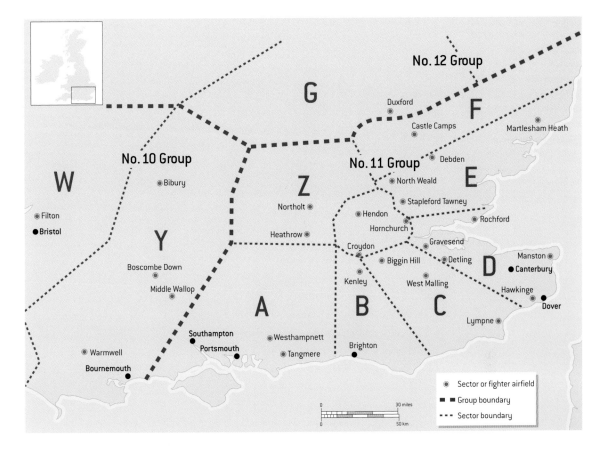

The Luftwaffe dubbed 13 August *Adlertag* ('Eagle Day'). It signalled the start of the second phase of the Battle of Britain: the sustained campaign against RAF airfields, radar stations and other key military targets such as aircraft and aero-engine factories. The bombers sent to strike at these targets were well escorted by both Bf 109Es and Bf 110s, and during 11 days of heavy raids, which saw both sides suffer terrible losses, the Luftwaffe began to assert its dominance through sheer weight of numbers.

In phase three, between 24 August and 6 September, German bomber units targeted Fighter Command airfields and aircraft factories, with growing success. The RAF would later call this 'the critical period' of the Battle of Britain, as it found it ever harder to replace losses. Yet despite suffering serious casualties – 217 Hurricane Is were destroyed in August alone – Fighter Command was still inflicting heavy losses on German forces. Indeed, the Bf 110 *Zerstörergruppen* had been so badly affected (with 93 aircraft destroyed between 13 and 31 August) that the role they would play in the rest of the campaign would be significantly reduced.

On 7 September, believing Fighter Command to be finished, Reichsmarschall Hermann Göring ordered his forces to target London instead in an effort to bring more RAF fighters into the air. Thus, the final, critical phase of the Battle of Britain commenced. Eventually the capital would be attacked both by day and night, culminating in two massive daylight raids on 15 September – immortalised thereafter by the British as Battle of Britain Day.

RAF Fighter Command sector and fighter airfields in southeast and southern England during the Battle of Britain.

A war photographer captured the activity at a forward base occupied by I./ZG 52 as the unit prepared to take off on another mission during the Battle of France. Here, 1. *Staffel*'s 'A2+BH' appears to be the lead aircraft.

By now the *Zerstörergruppen* were forbidden to fly their favoured *freie Jagd* sorties. Instead, Reichsmarschall Göring ordered them to provide close-formation escort for the bombers, which had suffered growing losses to the seemingly indestructible RAF. As if to prove that Fighter Command did indeed still have plenty of fight left in it, on 15 September both waves of bombers were met by close to 300 Hurricanes and Spitfires. The Bf 110 units played little part in the raids on this day, however, due to the horrendous losses they had suffered during the previous month. Indeed, only three aircraft were lost on 15 September. However, the month was topped and tailed by heavy casualties on 4 and 27 September when 16 and 19 Bf 110s were lost, respectively. At least 16 of these aircraft were downed by Hurricane Is.

September had seen Fighter Command endure a similarly high casualty rate as the Battle of Britain reached its climax, with some 210 Hurricane Is being destroyed in the air during the defence of southern England.

On 30 September the last massed daylight raids on London and the Southwest were flown, but the battered Bf 110 *Zerstörergeschwaders* were barely involved in the day's activities. Fighter Command was far from beaten: it inflicted heavy losses on the Luftwaffe formations, and on 12 October Operation *Sealion* was shelved. Five days earlier the Bf 110s had participated in their last major action over England when II. and III./ZG 26 were hard-hit while escorting Ju 88s that had been sent to attack the Westland aircraft works in Yeovil. Seven *Zerstörer* were downed by a mixed fighter force of Spitfires and Hurricanes.

The Battle of Britain officially ended on 31 October, by which time 223 Bf 110s had been lost in combat out of the 315 that had been committed to the campaign. The myth of the invincible bomber-destroyer had been graphically exposed to the point where *Zerstörer* would never again venture over Britain in such numbers.

THE COMBATANTS

The vast majority of the British and German fighter pilots who faced each other in 1940 were among the best-trained aviators to see combat in World War II. This was particularly true in the case of crews within the elite *Zerstörergruppen*; many had served with the Luftwaffe since its formation in the early 1930s and had been hand-picked to fly the new Bf 110. A number of these men came from single-seat *Jagdgeschwaders*, and some had seen combat in Bf 109s during the Spanish Civil War (1936–39). Fighter tactics trialled and perfected in action against Spanish Republican aircraft influenced the way the German fighter and *Zerstörer* forces trained and fought during the early years of World War II.

Although the pilots of RAF Fighter Command had no such combat experience to draw on, they were very well trained nevertheless thanks to constant drilling and exercises. As detailed in the previous chapter, the ground-control system in place in Britain was unmatched anywhere in the world, and fighter pilots were thoroughly trained in working with it.

With respect to the quality of the aircrew reaching the frontline, Fighter Command – as with the *Jagdwaffe* – only really began to feel the pinch during the latter stages of the Battle of Britain. At this point, heavy losses forced Training Command to cut corners in order keep units operational. By late 1940 the pilot supply crisis was over within the RAF, and training schemes in the UK and overseas – in South Africa, Southern Rhodesia, Australia, the USA and Canada – ensured that Fighter Command would never again suffer from a lack of personnel.

The Bf 110 represented a huge step up for pilots coming from the pedestrian Fw 58 and Ju 52/3m (which was also used as a training aircraft for students streamed onto multi-engine types). Consequently, this was a scene repeated with monotonous regularity at training bases across occupied Europe. Having possibly ground-looped either on take-off or landing, this Bf 110C-4 was damaged on 12 September 1940 at the *Zerstörerschule* at Prague-Rusin, Czechoslovakia.

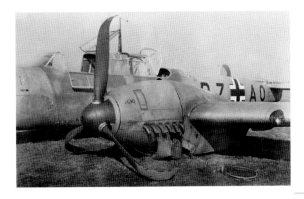

However, the same could not be said for the *Jagdwaffe*; as the war progressed, it struggled to replace lost aircrew. Although losses incurred during 1940 were swiftly made good, poor organisation of its training units eventually resulted in serious pilot shortages from 1943 onwards.

GERMAN PILOT TRAINING

Prior to the official creation of the Luftwaffe, all air activity in Germany had been geared towards training due to the ban on military flying under the terms of the 1919 Treaty of Versailles. Several quasi-military aviation organisations were formed in Germany during the late 1920s and early 1930s, functioning under the cover of civilian activities. Although the restrictions stalled the development of both combat aircraft and tactics, when the Luftwaffe was formed the focus on flying training provided it with plenty of military-trained aircrew. Men came from Lufthansa, gliding clubs and, until 1936, the Wehrmacht. However, the latter was expanding rapidly too, and eventually its senior officers forbade the Luftwaffe from recruiting from within the army. From then on, conscripts and volunteers would make up the numbers.

In Germany, pilot recruitment and training was strongly influenced by Prussian military tradition. Initially, future officers and NCOs alike could all expect to undertake six months of labour service, organised in a paramilitary fashion, with the *Reichsarbeitsdienst*. Those who were particularly air-minded chose service with the Party-controlled *Nationalsozialistisches Fliegerkorps* instead, flying gliders. However, with the Luftwaffe desperately short of personnel, labour service was reduced to just three months.

After induction into the Luftwaffe, all recruits spent between six and 12 months undertaking basic infantry training at a *Flieger-Ersatzabteilung* ('airman replacement battalion', FlErsAbt). Once recruits were deemed to be effective infantrymen, all were reviewed for possible advancement as pilots. Likely candidates were sent to a *Flug-Anwärterkompanie* ('aircrew candidate company', FlAnwKomp) for evaluation in a series of tests in basic aviation theory. For the next two months the applicants were tested on general aeronautical subjects, their instructors constantly assessing their suitability for possible advancement to a pilot training centre.

Those recruits deemed unsuitable for pilot training were redirected to a *Flieger-Ausbildungsregiment* ('airman development regiment', FlAR) for selection and introductory training in a branch more suited to their skills. In the case of the Bf 110 aircrew, these men may have reached the frontline as wireless operator/navigators and/or gunners. By

Bf 110 COCKPIT

1 Fuel cock levers

2 Seat adjustment handle

3 Throttle levers

4 Electrical system cut-out switch

5 Fuel system priming pump levers

6 Magneto switches

7 Undercarriage and flap emergency operation switches

8 Flap control switches

9 Air pressure gauge

10 Propeller pitch control levers

11 Undercarriage controls

12 Undercarriage position indicator

13 Cockpit illumination

14 Repeater compass

15 D/F control

16 Control column and gun firing button

17 Altimeter

18 Cannon rounds indicator

19 Machine gun rounds indicator with cocking switch below

20 Front cockpit locking levers

21 Turn and bank indicator

22 Revi gunsight

23 Artificial horizon

24 Port coolant temperature indicator

25 Fuel contents gauge

26 Starboard coolant temperature indicator

27 Coolant radiator flap position selector (port)

28 Fuel contents gauge selector switch

29 Coolant radiator flap position selector (starboard)

30 Airspeed indicator

31 Rate of climb indicator

32 Port propeller pitch indicator

33 Starboard propeller pitch indicator

34 Port R.P.M. indicator

35 Starboard R.P.M. indicator

36 Port boost gauge

37 Starboard boost gauge

38 Rudder pedals

39 Compass

40 Oxygen pressure gauge

41 Dimmer switch

42 Rudder trim control lever

43 Starter handles

44 Oxygen control

45 Spark plug cleaning handles

46 Selector lever for tank replenishing pump

47 Pilot's seat

48 Elevator trim control

following this process, the prospective aircrew candidate had already experienced some eight months of training prior to entering flight school.

Those selected for further training as potential aircrew then undertook the standard selection process within a FlAnwKomp, whereby the rest of their basic training, conducted over a period of three to four months, was completed alongside aircrew evaluation tests. The tests involved a more detailed examination of the candidate's abilities, including rigorous physical exercises (possibly using oxygen apparatus and a centrifuge) and progressively more challenging aeronautical theory. Indeed, the student's classroom work had to be of the highest standard or he would be scrubbed from the course and transferred to a FlErsAbt to complete his basic training, after which he would be allocated to another branch of the Luftwaffe.

Having got through initial induction and assessment, the *Flugzeugführer-Anwärter* ('pilot candidate') would receive instruction in basic flight theory and rudimentary aeronautics in a biplane trainer such as the Bücker Bü 131, Arado Ar 66C, Heinkel He 72 Kadett, Gotha Go 145 or Focke-Wulf FW 44 Stieglitz. Up to 60 circuits with an instructor was usually sufficient before the trainee was cleared to make his first flight. Those who failed to solo by 80 circuits were returned to a FlAR. Candidates were assessed for advancement throughout this phase, and those displaying the required aptitude would then be sent to *Flugzeugführerschule A/B* ('flight training school A/B') as soon as a space became available – typically two months after arriving at the FlAnwKomp. Here, flight training proper would be undertaken.

At such schools students passed through four principal levels of instruction, with each requiring qualification for its own licence before advancing to the next stage. The system of licences, which were earned over a period of six to nine months, explain the naming patterns of these flight schools. The *A1-Schein* ('A1 licence') introduced students to basic practical flying in dual-controlled training aircraft, with instructors teaching recruits how to take off and land, recover from stalls and attain a solo flight rating. Before the war and until early 1941, instructors would have been assigned four trainees each; however, the number rose as the conflict progressed.

For the *A2-Schein*, cadets were required to learn flight theory, including aerodynamics, meteorology, flying procedures and aviation law, as well as the practical application of aeronautical engineering, elementary navigation, wireless procedure and Morse code. In the air, they gained more flying experience on larger single-engined two-seat aircraft.

The next level of training, aimed at attaining the *B1-Schein*, saw pilots progress to high-performance single- and twin-engined machines typically fitted with a retractable undercarriage. If pilots were destined to fly fighters, at this stage older types of combat aircraft such as early-variant Bf 109s would be flown for the first time. Precision landing, night flying and night landing, and cross-country flying were all tested during this phase. The student pilot would also have to complete at least 50 flights in a *B1*-category aircraft. Upon gaining the *B1-Schein* – having accumulated 100 to 150 hours of flight time over the previous 14 to 17 months – students would undertake training aimed at acquiring the final *B2-Schein*.

These ZG 76 crewmen climbing aboard their machine using the aircraft's built-in retractable ladder are dressed in summer-weight *Kombination* K So/34 overalls. The point of interest illustrated here is the fact that *Zerstörer* pilots wore seat-pack *Sitzfallschirm* 30-IS-24B parachutes while Bordfunker were equipped with the backpack-type *Rückenfallschirm-12B*.

One of the key training types for would-be Bf 110 pilots was the humble Focke-Wulf Fw 58 Weihe, which was a true workhorse for the Luftwaffe. Designed as a six-seater civil transport and flown for the first time in the summer of 1935, it was quickly adopted by the Luftwaffe and used in a variety of roles including aircrew trainer. This particular example is an Fw 58B assigned to *Grosse Kampffliegerschulen* 4 at Thorn (Toruń), Poland, in 1940. The *Weihe* provided pilots with their first taste of flying a twin-engined type.

The A-licence course generally took three months to complete, with the B phase seeing pilots flying more advanced types. An elementary *K1 Kunstflug* ('stunt-flying') aerobatics course was also included in the latter phase to provide all pilots with a good understanding of rudimentary evasive manoeuvres (barrel rolls, loops and formation splits). This phase also allowed instructors to identify any potential fighter pilots among their students; thereafter, these candidates would receive more flying time than their fellow students.

Upon completion of the B2 phase, the cadet would finally be granted his *Luftwaffeflugzeugführerschein* ('air force pilots' licence'), accompanied by the highly prized *Flugzeugführerabzeichen* ('pilot's badge') – his 'wings'. After an average of ten to 13 months at a *Flugzeugführerschule A/B*, he was now a fully qualified pilot.

It was at this point that new aviators would be categorised for service on single- or multi-engined aircraft, with each individual assigned to a specialist flying school. Here, he would undergo intensive training for his allotted type. Those who showed sufficient mastery of twin-engined training aircraft such as the Fw 58 Weihe would be advanced to a *Flugzeugführerschule C* for an additional 50–70 hours on heavy aircraft over the next two to six months. Such pilots would ultimately serve with bomber, transport, reconnaissance or heavy-fighter ('destroyer') units.

Training at a *Flugzeugführerschule C* included an introduction to instrument flying and direction-finding apparatus on aircraft such as the Ju 52/3m transport. From here, pilots were split off and sent to appropriate specialist schools, with those selected for Bf 110s attending *Zerstörerschule* for two to three months of gunnery and target work.

Once at the *Zerstörerschule* pilots would be paired up with wireless operator/gunners, with whom they would continue service. This practice was maintained until the blood-letting of the Battle of Britain; at this point, a number of *Gruppen* (including III./ZG 76) began splitting up new replacement crews upon arrival at the frontline so that inexperienced pilots or wireless operator/gunners could fly their first few missions with 'old hands'. In training, *Zerstörerschule* crews would attend blind-flying school, then undertake an advanced instrument navigation course that included instrument flight, landing practice and advanced direction-finding techniques. Finally, having flown a total of some 220–270 hours in a multitude of aircraft types during a 20-month training course, the pilot and his wireless operator/gunner would finally join a frontline *Zerstörergruppe* as a reserve crew.

By 1940 the realities of war, with escalating attrition among aircrew, had led the Luftwaffe to modify the final stages of the training syllabus by creating *Ergänzungs*

(*Zerstörer*) *Staffel* ('[destroyer] operational training schools') for teaching tactics and for further familiarisation with frontline types. In the *Jagdwaffe*, such units were directly linked to and controlled by operational *Geschwaders*. The intention with these new units was to let new aircrew gain precious operational experience before being hurled into combat.

Like their pilots, the wireless operator/gunners in the *Zerstörergruppen* in 1940 had also received exhaustive training before being sent to an operational unit. Most had failed to make the grade as pilots but had shown enough aptitude to be sent from the FlAnwKomp to a *Beobachter-*, *Bordfunker*, *Bordmechanik-* or *Bordschützenschule* ('observer', 'wireless-operator', 'flight-engineer' or 'air-gunner school', respectively).

A Bordfunker in a Bf 110 was expected to be able to operate the radios, navigate proficiently and fire the rear-facing MG 15 machine gun effectively; he was therefore a skilled crewman. Indeed, by the time he reached the frontline he would have completed the nine-month basic wireless communication skills course at a *Luftnachrichtenschule* ('air communications school') that saw students attain a Morse-code speed of 100 letters a minute (for both reception and transmission), as well as master elementary navigation. Bordfunker also attended schools for actual flight practice and navigation, map-reading, radio-direction training and elementary aircraft engine instruction. Finally, they joined an air-gunnery school for a five-month course covering ground-based machine gun and other small-arms training, camera-gun practice aboard light trainer aircraft and air-to-air gunnery. After 16 to 18 months of hard graft during this gruelling course the successful Bordfunker would graduate, then be sent to a *Zerstörerschule* to team up with their new pilots and undertake two to three months of familiarisation training on the Bf 110. Only then were they deemed ready for combat.

BRITISH PILOT TRAINING

Between 1919 and 1936 the RAF was blighted by a lack of funding. However, eventually the overt re-arming of Germany prompted the government of the day to pay for the expansion that would be required to let the air force function effectively in a modern war. Central to this process was re-equipment, including the purchase of new single-seat monoplane fighters in the shape of the Hurricane and Spitfire. A large

An instructor from No. 8 EFTS vacates the back seat of Miles Magister I T9688 before sending a student pilot on his first solo flight at Woodley airfield, Berkshire. This aircraft had previously served with No. 5 EFTS at Hanworth, Middlesex, before joining No. 8 EFTS. The machine was destroyed in a raid on Woodley on 10 August 1940.

HURRICANE I COCKPIT

1 Radio contactor master switch
2 Cockpit light dimmer switch
3 Generator switch
4 Oil dilution pushbutton
5 Landing lamp control lever
6 Oxygen supply cock
7 R/T remote controller
8 Throttle control
9 Propeller speed control
10 Throttle lever friction adjuster
11 Landing lamp switch
12 Cockpit lights
13 Supercharger control
14 Fuel cock
15 Undercarriage emergency release lever
16 Rudder trim tab control

17 Elevator trim tab control
18 Radiator flap control lever
19 Hood catch control
20 Engine starter button
21 Booster coil push button
22 Boost control cut-out
23 Oxygen regulator
24 Clock
25 Undercarriage indicator on-off switch
26 Undercarriage indicator change-over switch
27 Undercarriage indicator
28 GM2 reflector gunsight
29 GM2 Reflector gunsight spare lamps
30 R.P.M. indicator
31 Reflector light switch
32 Boost gauge

33 Fuel tank selector switch
34 Fuel gauge
35 Fuel pressure warning light
36 Radiator temperature gauge
37 Oil pressure gauge
38 Gun camera switch
39 Navigation lights switch
40 Pressure head heater switch
41 Ignition switches
42 Fuel tank pressurising control
43 Oil temperature gauge
44 Cylinder priming pump
45 Signalling switch box
46 Emergency exit panel jettison lever
47 Hydraulic hand pump

48 Flap indicator
49 Seat adjustment lever
50 Undercarriage and flap selector lever
51 Pilot's seat
52 Control column and spade grip
53 Gun firing button
54 Compass
55 Rudder pedals
56 Windscreen de-icing pump
57 Airspeed indicator
58 Artificial horizon
59 Rate of climb indicator
60 Altimeter
61 Direction indicator
62 Turn and bank indicator
63 Brake pressure gauge

number of pilots would be needed on the frontline to fly these aircraft. It was obvious that the output of existing flying training schools (for short-service officers and airman pilots) and the RAF College at Cranwell (for permanent officers), at around 400 pilots a year, was grossly inadequate.

As part of the shake-up of the RAF instigated by the Air Ministry in 1936, which saw four specialist commands created in place of the Area Commands that had previously existed, Training Command was established. Three years before this the RAF had already taken steps to improve the flow of trained pilots by setting up a handful of civilian-manned elementary and reserve flying training schools (E&RFTSs), equipped with de Havilland Gipsy Moths, DH Tiger Moths and Blackburn B2s. That same year it had also set up a standardised training programme for future officer pilots at the RAF College.

Coinciding with the establishment of Training Command, the Air Ministry created the RAF Volunteer Reserve (RAFVR) with the aim of training 800 pilots a year. This scheme was open to all comers, no matter what their financial or social status, and it proved so popular that by 1940 a third of Fighter Command's pilots had originally joined as RAFVR members. A considerable number joined frontline units as sergeant pilots. Before this, all recruits would enter either as permanent or short-commission officers and NCOs, or via the Auxiliary Air Force. The latter, created in 1925, mirrored the Territorial Army in that units consisted of groups of men from particular geographical areas who would train together at weekends. These squadrons quickly ended up being manned by wealthy gentlemen, who set the tone for the auxiliaries into the early stages of World War II.

By late 1938, close to 30 E&RFTSs had been established, setting student pilots on the path to obtaining their wings through training on Tiger Moths, Miles Magisters and Blackburn B2s. An element of advanced training had also been introduced at these schools through the provision of Harts, Battles and Avro Ansons.

Pilots already serving in Fighter Command with operational units equipped with Gloster Gauntlet, Hawker Fury or Gloster Gladiator biplanes made the switch to the Hurricane or Spitfire at squadron level without the support of an operational conversion unit, since before the war such things did not exist. Initially, replacement of biplane fighters in the frontline proceeded at a leisurely pace due to production difficulties. However, the conversion process was dramatically speeded up following the Munich Crisis of September 1938. Had the latter escalated into war, the RAF's frontline fighter force would have struggled to defend southern England from attack by the Luftwaffe. The Air Ministry, determined to rectify this situation as quickly as possible, now implemented 'Master Plan M', which gave top priority to re-equipping Fighter Command. No. 43 Sqn was one unit that made the transition from Fury I to Hurricane I during this period, as future ace Flg Off Peter Townsend recalled in his autobiography, *Duel of Eagles*:

The 'catching-up' process started on 29 November 1938 with the arrival of Hurricanes L1725 and L1727 at Tangmere. By mid-December we had our full initial equipment of 16 aircraft. The Fury had been a delightful plaything; the Hurricane was a thoroughly war-like machine, rock solid as a platform for its eight Browning machine guns, highly manoeuvrable despite its large proportions and with an excellent view from the cockpit. At first the Hurricane earned a bad reputation. The change from the light and agile Fury caught some pilots unaware. The Hurricane was far less tolerant of faulty handling, and a mistake at low altitude could be fatal. There were certain problems with the Merlin engines too, as we occasionally experienced a phenomenon known as 'surging', accompanied by a sudden loss of power. This problem, and others, was quickly cured, however, and we soon came to know ourselves and our Hurricanes better. There grew in us a trust and an affection for them and their splendid Merlin engines, thoroughbreds and stayers which changed our fearful doubts of the Munich period into the certainty that we could beat all comers.

All our flying at this time was designed to gird us for war, which was bound to come: battle climbs to 30,000ft, where the engine laboured and the controls were sluggish and we inhaled the oxygen which came hissing into our face-masks from a black steel cylinder behind the armoured bulkhead; air drill and practice attacks and firing our guns into the sea, where they raised a jagged plume of foam. The recoil of those eight Brownings could slow the aircraft in a climb by 40mph; cloud flying and night flying, which no one really enjoyed.

Quick refuelling and re-arming practice gave groundcrews the sleight of hand which speeded their tasks and gained precious seconds. Between them and the pilots existed an understanding on which our lives depended. The slightest grumble from an engine, or any other functional defect – it might occur five miles above the ground or ten miles from the coast – had to be explained to our fitters or riggers, or to the armourers and radio mechanics, in the terms and nuances of their technical language. We could provide the clue but we relied implicitly on their vigilance, skill and devotion to keep our machines free of defects which could cost us our lives.

For those trainee aviators who entered the RAF's revised pilot training system in 1938, the first steps on the way to achieving one's wings usually took the form of an *ab initio* flying course at an E&RFTS, which typically lasted three months. Once this had been successfully completed, the student was accepted into the RAF. Towards the end of this three-month period pilots where asked to make a choice as to whether they wanted to fly bombers or fighters.

Following graduation from the E&RFTS, pilots destined to be commissioned then spent two weeks undergoing officer training at RAF Uxbridge, where they were fitted with uniforms, before heading to a flying training school (FTS). At the FTS students would typically fly Hart biplanes in their junior term, and on completion of this phase they were awarded their pilots' 'wings'. Fury fighters – at that time still very much in

Hurricane Is of No. 85 Sqn in tight battle formation over Kent during the Battle of Britain. The rigid adherence to such unwieldy tactics by Fighter Command throughout 1940 saw Hurricane I and Spitfire units sustain heavy losses to both Bf 109Es and Bf 110s conducting their favoured 'dive-and-zoom' attacks from superior altitude.

JOHN IGNATIUS KILMARTIN

Although ten RAF pilots claimed five or more Bf 110s destroyed flying the Hurricane I in 1940, the leading *Zerstörer* killer during this period was Flg Off John 'Killy' or 'Iggie' Kilmartin. He claimed all bar one of his seven Bf 110 victories in France with No. 1 Sqn between 11 and 17 May, the final victory coming on 6 September after Kilmartin had been transferred to No. 43 Sqn.

Born in Dundalk in what is now Eire on 8 July 1913, Kilmartin was one of eight children. His father, a forester, died when Kilmartin was just nine years old, and he was duly shipped to Australia under a scheme known as 'Big Brother'. Once old enough, Kilmartin found work on a cattle station in New South Wales, where he remained for five years in the early 1930s. After joining an aunt in Shanghai, China, he worked as a clerk in the accounts department of the Shanghai Gas Works for more than two years until in 1936 he saw an advertisement for short-service commission applicants for the RAF. Having received a positive response to his letter of application, Kilmartin came to the UK via the trans-Siberian railway.

Taught to fly at a civilian school in Perthshire, Scotland, he was accepted into the RAF in February 1937 and sent to No. 6 FTS at Netheravon. Having gained his wings, later that year he joined No. 43 Sqn at Tangmere, which was equipped with Fury Is. Promoted to squadron adjutant in September 1939, Kilmartin volunteered for service with No. 1 Sqn in France two months later. He claimed a half-share in a Do 17 on 23 November 1939, a Bf 109E on 2 April 1940 and a Ju 88 18 days later. He was subsequently involved in the fighting in northeast France in the wake of the German invasion on 10 May 1940. Indeed, Kilmartin claimed a shared Do 17 on that date, two Bf 110s on 11 May, an 'He 112' (actually a Bf 109E) the following day, two more Bf 109Es on the 14 May, single Bf 110s on 15 and 16 May and two more on 17 May.

Returning to Britain at month's end, Kilmartin served as an instructor with Nos. 6 and 5 OTUs until August 1940, when he rejoined No. 43 Sqn as a flight commander. He claimed his final two victories with this unit on 6 and 7 September when he downed a Bf 110 and a Bf 109E, respectively. Awarded the Distinguished Flying Cross the following month, Kilmartin held various command positions for the rest of the war; these included serving as CO of No. 602 Sqn in April 1941, supernumerary to help form No. 313 'Czech' Sqn later that year, CO of No. 128 Sqn in west Africa in 1942 and CO of No. 504 Sqn in 1943. Promoted to wing commander, Kilmartin led the Hornchurch Wing and was then made Wing Commander Ops of No. 84 Wing in late 1943. Commanding No. 136 Wing at Normandy in 1944, he finished the war as Wing Leader of No. 910 Wing in Burma.

Kilmartin remained in the RAF after the war, again holding various positions of command, including CO of No. 249 Sqn for 18 months in Iraq. Retiring from the service in July 1958, he settled in Devon and ran a chicken farm for 15 years before travelling through Europe for almost a decade. Returning to Devon in 1984, Kilmartin died on 1 October 1998.

service with Fighter Command – awaited them in their senior term. Completing nine months of flying training, the brand-new fighter pilot was duly posted to a frontline unit within Fighter Command.

For a pilot fresh from an FTS, where he had flown obsolescent biplane fighters that boasted just two guns and barely reached 200mph, the step up to a monoplane

HANS-JOACHIM JABS

Only two *Zerstörer* pilots officially claimed enough kills in 1940 to be rated as aces against the Hurricane I, although a number of their contemporaries may have achieved this feat by erroneously claiming Spitfires as their victims rather than the Hawker fighter. Oberleutnant Hans-Joachim Jabs and Hauptmann Heinz Nacke of 6./ZG 76 were credited with destroying five Hurricanes apiece, as well as a handful of Spitfires, over France and southern England during the spring and summer of 1940.

Born in Lübeck on 14 November 1917, Jabs joined the Luftwaffe in 1936 and was originally trained to fly the Bf 109. However, in March 1940 he was transferred to II./ZG 76, equipped with Bf 110Cs, at Cologne-Wahn. Finding himself in the thick of the action from the very start of the *Blitzkrieg*, Jabs claimed a French Curtiss Hawk 75 destroyed on 12 May and a Morane-Saulnier MS.406 the following day. Another MS.406 fell to his guns during the afternoon of 15 May, and he 'made ace' exactly two weeks later with two 'Spitfire' kills – although these were almost certainly Hurricane Is from No. 151 Sqn. Jabs claimed an MS.406 on 7 June, followed by a Spitfire and a Hurricane during the bloody clashes of 15 August. Another Hurricane was downed on 30 August and a Spitfire 24 hours later. On 1 September Jabs claimed a Spitfire and two Hurricanes destroyed while defending Do 17s of KG 76 that had been sent to bomb Biggin Hill, and 72 hours later he was credited with two Spitfires and a Hurricane destroyed while escorting Bf 110Ds of Erpr. Gr. 210 during their attack on the Vickers-Armstrong aircraft factory near Weybridge. Jabs's final claims in 1940 took the form of two more Spitfires on 7 and 11 September.

Jabs's achievements earned him the Knight's Cross and promotion to Oberleutnant on 1 October 1940. Jabs would claim one more kill flying with ZG 76, taking his tally to 20, before retraining as a nightfighter pilot in late 1941 and joining *Nachtjagdgeschwader* (NJG) 3 in the defence of Hamburg. It was only after he transferred to NJG 1 in Holland that his score began to rise again, and by the time he was made *Kommodore* of the unit in March 1944, his tally stood at 44. At this time Jabs was awarded the Oak Leaves to the Knight's Cross. Proving that old habits die hard, the following month he claimed a brace of Spitfire IXs near his Arnhem-Deelen base in broad daylight while returning home in his Bf 110G following a night patrol. Although his fighter was also shot up in the engagement, Jabs survived unscathed. His final successes came on the night of 21 February 1945, when he downed two Lancasters to take his final tally to 50 victories – 22 day and 28 night kills.

One of the highest-scoring Bf 110 aces to survive the war, by VE-Day Jabs had completed 710 missions. After the war he moved to Lüdenscheid and ran a prosperous business selling heavy agricultural machinery. Hans-Joachim Jabs died on 23 October 2003.

fighter such as the Hurricane I, with eight guns and a top speed of more than 300mph, was a huge one. In an effort to fill the yawning performance gap, the RAF established several Group Pools in 1939 and equipped them with a handful of Hurricanes and Spitfires. Here, new pilots would be able to get a precious few flying hours on their logbooks on-type before they joined Fighter Command proper.

With the declaration of war, all E&RFTSs were brought within the RAF Training Command structure as Elementary FTSs (EFTSs). Once finished at an EFTS, pupils

All four of these Masters, seen performing a low-level formation fly-by for the press at Sealand, south of Liverpool, in late 1940, are being flown by future No. 71 'Eagle' Sqn pilots. Assigned to No. 5 FTS, aircraft '29' (N7760), '18' (N7765) and '11' (N7691) were standard unarmed two-seat Master Is, while '27' (N7820) was one of a small number of Miles advanced trainers fitted with six 0.303-in machine guns and converted into single-seat 'emergency' fighters at the height of the Battle of Britain. Fortunately, they were never needed in the frontline, but they were retained within Fighter Command as aerial gunnery trainers well into 1942.

would progress to Service FTSs (SFTSs), which by early 1940 had been boosted in number from six to 11. The aircraft types operated at both stages in the training process remained much the same during the first 18 months of the war, although the interwar biplane fighters encountered at the SFTSs slowly began to be replaced by North American Harvard Is and the all-new Miles Master.

The Group Pool system allowed operational squadrons to draw replacement pilots from a pool and therefore relinquish their own training responsibilities so they could concentrate on combat missions. However, in wartime the system soon started to show signs of strain. Indeed, literally thousands of trainee pilots – many with a considerable number of flying hours already in their logbooks – were transferred to other trades in late 1939 and early 1940 due to a chronic shortage of monoplane fighter types within the Group Pools. Spitfires and Hurricanes were urgently needed on the frontline, leaving no aircraft for training purposes.

In the early spring of 1940, all Group Pools were redesignated operational training units (OTUs) within Training Command, and the Air Ministry instructed Fighter Command to ensure that enough aircraft were made available to these units so that a steady flow of replacement pilots could be sent through them. The OTUs eventually succeeded where the Group Pools had failed thanks to an influx of often combat-weary fighter aircraft, along with equally battle-seasoned staff for instructing would-be frontline pilots. Among such staff was future ace Flg Off Billy Drake, who had just recovered from wounds sustained when his No. 1 Sqn Hurricane I was shot down by a Bf 110 over France on 13 May 1940. Drake was sent to No. 6 OTU at Sutton Bridge in June 1940, as recounted in his autobiography *Billy Drake: Fighter Leader*.

Prior to the war, most advanced training of fighter pilots had taken place at unit level – as had been my own experience. The demands of war made this difficult to continue with, and soon after the outbreak of hostilities specialised training units had been set up to raise pilots' experience to a point where – theoretically at least – they were ready to play their full part as soon as they joined an operational squadron.

However, June 1940 found Fighter Command reeling from the losses over France and the Dunkirk evacuation, facing imminent onslaught by the Luftwaffe and desperate for additional pilots at the earliest possible date. Products of the Volunteer Reserve, partly trained at the outbreak of war, were now completing a foreshortened and hasty advanced training, whilst the first foreign pilots who had escaped from the shambles in France were also being made ready to join British units.

For me this period at No. 6 OTU remains in my memory as one of bloody hard work. I flew my arse off, 40–50 hours a month. My job was to firstly make certain that these new pilots could actually fly, and for this purpose I went aloft with them in Master and Harvard advanced trainers. When satisfied that this was the case, I would send them off in Hurricanes, accompanying them in my own aircraft firstly to see if they could fly formation, and then to try and teach them the rudiments of dogfighting. Almost incredibly, with the benefit of hindsight, no provision existed for them to obtain any instruction or experience of aerial gunnery at this stage of the war.

Fellow future ace Flt Lt Johnny Kent attended the No. 7 OTU system at Hawarden in July 1940, prior to being posted to No. 303 'Polish' Sqn at the end of that same month. A pre-war fighter and test pilot and a veteran of photo-reconnaissance missions over Germany in unarmed Spitfires early in the war, Kent reinforced Drake's incredulous views on the lack of gunnery training given to pilots passing through the OTU system in 1940 in his autobiography, *One of the Few*:

Everything was confused during this period and the training syllabus was very sketchy – it consisted mainly of formation flying and dogfighting exercises. I kept asking my flight commander, Flt Lt Bill Kain (also a Hurricane I veteran of France, where he served with No. 73 Sqn), about air firing, explaining that I had never fired eight guns and I wanted to find out what they sounded like – and what effect they had on the aircraft.

Finally, in desperation, he allowed me one shoot. My target was a spit of sand in the Dee Estuary and, on my first attack, I got a neat group with a half-second burst, but on my second dive the guns failed to fire. I tried several more times but nothing happened so, in a bit of a temper, I returned to the airfield and told Bill Kain what I thought of an installation which could produce stoppages in all eight guns at once. Bill then explained that there had been no stoppage – that was all the ammunition they could spare me!

I knew that both the country and the Air Force were in a pretty bad way, but this brought home to me just how desperate the situation was. It did not matter so much in my particular case as I had done so much front-gun firing before, although it was only with two guns, but many of the new boys never fired their guns at all until they went into action for the first time – a sobering thought when one considers the task before them. It was a great tribute to their grit and determination that they carried themselves into the violent battles of the next few months, and inflicted the damage they did, with virtually no instruction or practice in air-firing at all. One wonders what the results might have been if it had been possible to thoroughly train every pilot before he went into action.

When losses began to mount in August 1940 , OTU courses for new pilots were drastically shortened from several months to just four weeks, leaving squadrons to apply the finishing touches. As a result of this, Fighter Command began receiving replacement pilots who had never even seen a Spitfire or Hurricane, let alone mastered them in flight, and who had received little more than basic training in blind or night flying, navigation or gunnery.

Despite cutting corners in pilot training, still more men were needed as replacements because the Luftwaffe was continuing to exact a heavy toll on the RAF. With no time to train pilots from scratch, Fighter Command sought out men from other commands within the RAF, as well as the Fleet Air Arm. The best pilots from Army Cooperation, Coastal and Bomber Commands were posted in, as were 75 partly trained naval pilots. Combat-seasoned fighter pilots also came from Poland, Czechoslovakia, Belgium and France, these men having fled to Britain following the Nazi occupation of their respective countries.

These were the sort of men who manned the 31 Hurricane I squadrons that helped defend Britain in the summer of 1940. Their experiences are detailed in the next chapter.

COMBAT

Prior to the launch of the *Blitzkrieg* in the West on 10 May 1940 Hurricane Is and Bf 110s had clashed on only four occasions during the Phoney War. The first engagement, between No. 73 Sqn and 13. and 15.(Z)/LG 1 on 26 March 1940, had ended inconclusively (although three Bf 110Cs force-landed with damage), but three days later No. 1 Sqn succeeded in destroying a machine from 14.(Z)/LG 1. Flg Off Paul Richey of No. 1 Sqn recalled:

Johnny Walker got the first Messerschmitt 110 to fall to Allied fighters. With Bill Stratton and 'Darky' Clowes he sighted nine of them, the first to appear over France, north of Metz.

The Hurricanes climbed to attack. Johnny stuck behind one through some violent manoeuvres and first-class flying – vertical stall turns and so on. He followed it through cloud, saw it catch fire and ran out of ammunition. It was later found in pieces, the pilot having bailed out – the gunner was killed.

Air Marshal 'Ugly' Barratt, who commanded the British air forces in France, had a few days previously issued an invitation to dine with him in Paris to the first pilot to shoot down a Messerschmitt 110 on the Western Front. The Air Marshal's personal aircraft collected Johnny, Stratton and Clowes the day after their successful engagement with the 110s. The Air Marshal turned on a slap-up dinner at Maxim's for them – quite rightly, I thought.

This initial victory marked the start of No. 1 Sqn's outstanding success against the Bf 110, the unit proving to be the nemesis of Göring's 'Ironsides' throughout the Battle of France. The excellent results achieved in aerial combat by No. 1 Sqn both during the Phoney War and the French débâcle that followed were due in no small part to modified gun harmonisation and tactics that the unit had adopted unofficially. With respect to the former, before the war all squadrons of single-seat eight-gun

aircraft in Fighter Command had been instructed to use the 'Dowding Spread', this method of gun harmonisation being officially laid down in response to Air Marshal Dowding's conviction that his fighters would not see, let along engage, enemy fighters. In theory, the 'spread' made sense when attacking formations of bombers from astern, as it produced a wide enough pattern of bullets to compensate for aiming error, while still leaving sufficient lethal density to destroy targets of such size. The harmonisation range was set at 400yd, which also left the RAF fighters beyond the effective striking distance of enemy gunners defending the bombers.

However, in early 1939 the pilots of No. 1 Sqn realised that the spread was unsuitable for air fighting, as Flg Off Richey explained:

> We reckoned that even if the experts were right and that at 400 yards' range the bullet velocity was still high enough to prevent tumble, maintain accuracy and penetrate armour (which seemed unlikely), the spread produced by aiming, shooting and random errors combined would be more than enough to drop lethal density below the minimum required for a kill, especially against a small target like a fighter – which *we* were not at *all* convinced we would never meet. Fighter Command dismissed our theories, so during our month's shooting practice in the spring of 1939 we secretly harmonised all our guns on a spot at 250 yards' range. We shot the towed banner clean away time and time again. Our early action in France had now proved the point – we had shot down every aircraft we had attacked. All single-seat fighter squadrons were instructed to adopt our method. It was not a moment too soon.

Fighter Command tactics in the early stages of World War II have also come in for much criticism over the years, the RAF rigidly implementing unwieldy Fighting Area Attacks that could trace their origin to the early 1930s. At that time, the sole purpose of the British fighter element was seen as stopping formations of enemy bombers from attacking the UK. The fighters built throughout this decade – both biplane and monoplane – possessed limited range, and with France as an ally it was assumed that no enemy fighters would be able to reach British airspace, so bombers would be forced to attack unescorted. The Air Staff also believed that with monoplane fighters now capable of achieving speeds of more than 300mph, pilots would black out if they attempted to dogfight.

At this time RAF fighters were armed exclusively with rifle-calibre 0.303-in machine guns; the weight of fire of these weapons was deemed insufficient to bring down bombers

flying in tight, massed formations, when fighters attacked independently of one another. The RAF's Air Fighting Development Establishment therefore decided that the only way to solve this problem was to mass fighters in close formation so as to bring a large number of guns to bear.

Pilots in frontline fighter units were well drilled in formation flying, so a series of six basic patterns known as Fighting Area Attacks were duly

Another shot of No. 85 Sqn in battle formation, climbing hard over Kent in the summer of 1940. The unit's CO, Sqn Ldr Peter Townsend, described these formation tactics in his autobiography *Duel of Eagles*: 'I must admit I had qualms about leading my little band into the midst of a vast horde of the enemy. For this is how we fought – independently in squadrons of 12 aircraft. We had often discussed among ourselves how to go about it; our job was to go for the bombers. It was the Spitfires' job to look for the enemy fighter escort. Only if they barred the way would we mix it with them. I led No. 85 in four sections of three, each section in line astern, my own in the centre, one on each side, one behind, and each at a comfortable distance. The squadron had a narrow front and was easy to manoeuvre. Each pilot was able to search.'

formulated and published in the RAF *Manual of Air Tactics*, released in 1938. They were at the heart of standard squadron air drills; pilots strove to achieve perfection in formation, with a view to ensuring the success of the flight and squadron attacks that were so regularly practised. The order to attack was always preceded by the flight commander designating the number of the attack – for example, 'Fighting Area Attack No. 5 – go.' These attacks provided wonderful training in formation drill, but were worthless in terms of any relationship with effective shooting. Pilots complained that there was never enough time to get the gunsight on the target because they were too preoccupied with keeping station with the aircraft all around them.

The standard RAF fighter formation at the time was the V-shaped 'Vic' of three aircraft. A squadron of 12 fighters would be split into two flights, 'A' and 'B', each in turn comprising two sections of three fighters. When in full-strength battle formation, all 12 aircraft would be tightly grouped together in four sections of three fighters. Leading the Vic would be the squadron CO or senior flight commander, with succeeding 'Vs' following in close line astern. Once bombers had been spotted, the commander would position his formation behind them and then lead the attack in section after section.

Such attacks would have worked well against German bombers had it not been for the presence of escort fighters sweeping the skies ahead of them. *Jagdwaffe* tactics, as discussed in detail later in this chapter, were far more flexible in nature, and centred on smaller formations engaging other fighters rather than just bombers. As RAF Fighter Command would soon find out to its cost, Fighting Area Attacks were useless against small formations of high-performance fighters – especially Bf 109Es. Indeed when the German pilots, who invariably enjoyed a height advantage, observed the British fighters flying into combat in tight, neat rows of three, they quickly gave the Vics their own name: '*Idiotenreihen*' ('rows of idiots').

Those pilots who survived their initial encounters with the enemy soon came to realise that a combat formation had to be able to manoeuvre while maintaining cohesion. Pilots also had to be able to cover each other's blind areas so as to prevent surprise attacks on the formation. Finally, individual members of the formation had to be able to support each other should they come under attack.

The Luftwaffe's four-strong *Schwarm* formation (based on the loose pair, or *Rotte*, which was at the heart of all *Jagdwaffe* formations) met all these criteria, but Fighter Command's tight Vics did not. A *Schwarm* could turn as tightly as any individual aircraft within the formation, whereas the Vic's rate of turn was limited by the need for it to pivot on the aircraft on the inside of the turn.

When looking for the enemy, all the members of the looser *Schwarm* enjoyed the freedom to search the skies (and cover blind areas astern of the formation) without fear of running into a wingman. In the Vic, only the leader could search for the enemy, as his two wingmen had to concentrate on remaining in tight formation. This left them highly susceptible to attack from behind and below, and in 1940 this blind spot was repeatedly exploited by the *Jagdwaffe*.

Finally, if a *Rotte* or *Schwarm* was attacked from behind, a quick turn by the formation would see the attacker immediately come under threat himself. If the rear section of an RAF formation were bounced, the aircraft under attack had usually been shot down well before another pilot could attempt to fend off the enemy fighters.

'Sharksmouths' of II./ZG 76 overfly the smoking ruins of Dunkirk in early June 1940. The BEF has been forced into evacuation and the first half of the Battle of France has been won. The *Gruppe* lost three Bf 110s to RAF fighters during Operation *Dynamo*, but claimed 28 Spitfires and two Hurricane Is destroyed in return.

Although frontline units quickly realised how vulnerable fighting area attacks left them to German fighters, Vic formations would remain the norm well into 1941. Indeed, officially pilots were forbidden from implementing new tactics at unit level, as the RAF *Manual of Air Tactics* of 1938 stated 'Squadron Commanders are not to practice forms of attack other than those laid down, unless they have been specially authorised by Headquarters, Fighter Command.'

Even though in the spring of 1940 a serious flaw in RAF tactics had been cruelly exposed, there was really no time for Fighter Command to rectify this problem by issuing new tactics on the eve of the Battle of Britain. In a bid to improve the operability of the Vic, Fighter Command permitted squadrons to widen out the formations, thus allowing pilots to search the skies for the enemy more freely, rather than concentrating on close formation-keeping with the lead aircraft. A section or pair of aircraft would also now fly as 'weavers' some 1,000ft above and behind the main formation in an effort to forestall surprise attacks from the rear. This change in tactics was again prompted by the success of No. 1 Sqn, which was in a better position to ignore Fighter Command directives because the unit was no longer under the command's jurisdiction in France. Flg Off Richey recalled:

We all took it in turns to be designated 'arse-end-Charlie'. He was the chap who hung about above and behind the formation, which was usually in open 'Vic'. His job was to protect the formation's tail, which was blind when flying straight, and to prevent a surprise attack. We had learned this technique from the French soon after our arrival in eastern France, and usually had two 'Charlies', who proved indispensable. In fact, not once during the entire campaign in France was our formation surprised. We were often attacked from above, which is a different matter; but we always saw the enemy before he was in range and were never jumped.

However, without anyone to protect their tails, countless 'weavers' were themselves shot down during the Battle of Britain. These modifications certainly improved the

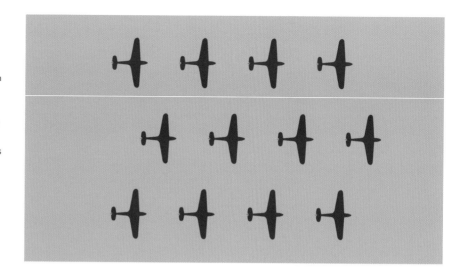

search and mutual-support capabilities of Fighter Command's formations, but did nothing to improve their ability to perform tight turns without losing cohesion.

Throughout the Battle of France, RAF Hurricane units would routinely encounter Bf 110s as the latter flew ahead of German bomber formations, attempting to sweep the skies clear of Allied fighters. Other *Zerstörer* would remain with the bombers, providing close escort. The actions on 11 May set the tone for the rest of the month when Nos. 73 and 501 Sqns engaged Bf 110Cs from I./ZG 2 that were escorting He 111Hs from II./KG 53. No. 1 Sqn's 'B' Flight was intercepted by additional elements of I./ZG 2 while protecting Battles. That same evening No. 1 Sqn's 'A' Flight took on I./ZG 26 as it escorted Do 17Zs from III./KG 76.

As would be the case during the spring and summer of 1940, the Hurricane I pilots were heavily outnumbered on each occasion (often by as many as three-to-one), yet they used the superior manoeuvrability of their aircraft to inflict losses on both the escorts and the bombers.

Two Hurricane Is were lost to the *Zerstörergruppen* and four Bf 110s shot down, as well as 14 German bombers. Overclaiming was rife on both sides, however, and this too became an enduring theme of the air war in 1940. Indeed, Hurricane I pilots were credited with the destruction of 18 Bf 110s on 11 May! Further heavy claims were made four days later, when pilots from four units were credited with 13 *Zerstörer* destroyed, and on 18 May when 21 Bf 110s were shared by nine squadrons. *Zerstörergruppen* losses for *both* days amounted to 21 aircraft.

From the very start of the *Blitzkrieg*, British fighter pilots reported that *Zerstörergruppen* would quickly form up into a defensive circle as soon as they spotted them. This tactic had been devised

The defensive circle (*Abwehrkreis*, in Luftwaffe parlance) was routinely adopted by Bf 110 units in combat throughout 1940. It had two potential aims. First, it was a defensive manoeuvre, with the forward guns of each aircraft protecting the tail of the aircraft ahead. Second, it allowed a formation to effectively take possession of an extensive area of sky which could then be occupied and defended for as long as necessary – when covering the approach or withdrawal of another formation, for example. When used in the latter fashion the tactic lured enemy fighters to attack a potentially lethal formation at some disadvantage.

by the original *Lehrgruppe* as the Bf 110's best means of defence against a more manoeuvrable opponent; the circle was laid down in every *Zerstörer* pilot's handbook. Over the next few months references to the term 'circle' would also appear with increasing frequency in RAF fighter pilots' after-action combat reports, as embattled Bf 110s resorted to it more and more.

The reasoning behind this manoeuvre is explained in detail by leading Luftwaffe historians John Vasco and Peter Cornwall in their book *Zerstörer*:

> The circular formation adopted by Bf 110s and often referred to by British pilots was not always an entirely defensive manoeuvre. The idea that up to 30 *Zerstörers* would automatically protect themselves from attack by five Hurricanes in this way reflects the relative naivety of some of the younger, more inexperienced, RAF pilots of the time. Yet this notion clearly improved their confidence when facing such odds. The more provocative use of the defensive circle led to its being renamed the *Angriffskreis* or 'attack circle' which, it was later argued, had a more confident ring to it. Later, with the grim humour common in any air force, some *Zerstörer* pilots came to call it the *Angstkreis* or 'circle of fear' – their schoolgirl shrieks down the radio as they circled around prompted angry rebukes from the *Kommandeur*.

Hurricane I pilots were dismissive of the defensive circle, as they quickly realised that that they could either dive on it or break into it and use their tighter turning

radius to pick off the Bf 110s from inside it. The circle also had to be complete for it to work at all, and if it was formed too slowly it could easily be attacked. Charles Gardner, a BBC correspondent in France, witnessed pilots from No. 1 Sqn successfully get inside a defensive circle during the great aerial clashes of 15 May:

There was a fight before breakfast when a section of Hurricanes ran into 15 Me 110s, of which seven or eight straightaway adopted 'circus tactics' – that is, revolving on each other's tail. This was one of the first indications that the 110s were wary of Hurricanes, and preferred to adopt defensive measures rather than offensive ones. This characteristic of 110 formations still persists, and when attacked, they almost always invariably form the old defensive ring. On this occasion the Hurricanes climbed round into one run and then broke into the German formation, one after the other. Two 110s went down – one without part of its tail and the other giving out smoke and steam.

The Battle of France quickly revealed that the Bf 110 could not hope to 'mix it' with the Hurricane I in a dogfight. This confirmed the fears of Oberleutnant Victor Mölders of 1./ZG 1, who commented 'The Bf 110 was not manoeuvrable. The steering was too heavy. In tight turns it slid about and fell out of the sky like a leaf from a tree. Trimming the aircraft or increasing speed didn't help.' Leutnant Richard Marchfelder of II./ZG 1 noted gloomily "After our first encounter with British fighters it became soberly clear to us that the holidays were over and we had to use all of our wits to fight a desperate enemy.'

Yet despite taking heavy losses between 11 May and 3 June (around 80 Bf 110s were destroyed in combat, but not all by Hurricane Is), the *Zerstörergruppen* had in the main achieved what had been demanded of them – long-range bomber escort. The Bf 110s had routinely operated from bases far behind the frontline, and their superior range and endurance had proven invaluable when it came to protecting vulnerable bomber formations from Allied fighters. When flown by an experienced pilot, the *Zerstörer* had shown that it could hold its own against most types, including the

Hurricane I. And even when Spitfires were encountered for the first time over Dunkirk, certain German pilots still believed in the fighting abilities of their bomber-destroyer. As Vasco and Cornwall point out, 'Those who flew the Bf 110 with some flair and a certain élan, and in combat situations invariably flat out at full emergency boost, had no such qualms.'

One of the Bf 110's great strengths was its speed when diving. Hurricane I pilots often commenting that they could not stay with the enemy aircraft when it pushed its nose down. No. 151 Sqn CO and future ace Sqn Ldr Teddy Donaldson experienced this at first hand on 18 May while attempting to engage Bf 110Cs from II./ZG 76:

I pulled the plug (engine boost) and climbed after two Messerschmitt 110s which were the remains of six that had just escorted Do 17s sent to bomb our airfield at Vitry. When I climbed to 6,000ft the Messerschmitts attacked. They passed vertically down behind me and I was able to flick-roll in behind one of them, which dived to ground level into the smoke of the burning Hurricanes at Vitry. I followed, pulled the plug, but although I was doing well over 400mph, I could not gain on him.

Bf 110 pilots, like their Bf 109E brethren, had shown a liking for 'dive-and-zoom' attacks during the Battle of France, with the bomber-destroyer able to make use of its superior armament in such scenarios. This tactic worked well when the *Zerstörergruppen* had a height advantage, and in May 1940 this was typically the case. For example, on the last day of the month over the Dunkirk beaches, three Bf 110Cs from 5./ZG 26 dived at full speed on a formation of close to 50 Hurricane Is and Spitfires as it patrolled off the French coast. Targeting the 'weavers' at the rear of the formation, the *Zerstörer* pilots picked off two Hurricane Is from No. 229 Sqn on their first pass. The Bf 110s then regained height using the speed built up in their dive while the British fighters milled around below, getting in each others' way due to the rigidity of their battle formation. Taking advantage of this, the *Zerstörer* made two more passes and claimed three Spitfires destroyed before discretion got the better of them and they made good their escape.

Missions such as this one went a long way to restoring the morale of the *Zerstörergruppen* which, despite having taken a battering from Allied fighters, were still confident of securing control of the skies over England following the capitulation of France.

BATTLE OF BRITAIN

The recent advance of the *Zerstörer* to the Channel coast had clearly shown up chinks in the Bf 110's armour, and operations over southern England during what would become known as the Battle of Britain would shatter the reputation of Göring's 'Ironsides'. However, the Hurricane I units that would oppose the *Zerstörergruppen*, and the rest of the all-conquering Luftwaffe, had taken a mighty beating in their ill-fated defence of France. Some 386 aircraft had been either shot down or abandoned

OVERLEAF
At 0745hrs on 15 May 1940, a large formation of Bf 110Cs (possibly from I./ZG 26) overflew Berry-au-Bac airfield at 15,000ft. They formed part of the escort for bombers sent to attack Laon. Six Hurricane Is from No. 1 Sqn's 'B' Flight were scrambled, with Flt Lt Peter Prosser Hanks leading the chase in N2380. The Hurricanes were unable to catch the Bf 110 formation until the latter changed direction. Hanks later recalled: 'We got above them and I dived vertically on the leader and fired a burst, allowing deflection, and he just blew up. Nothing left of him but a few small pieces.' Hanks shot down a second Bf 110 moments later, but his own fighter was badly hit and he was forced to bail out of the blazing aircraft.

Epitomising the spirit of *freie Jagd*, this unidentified machine of ZG 26 hunts among the scattered clouds. The crews of aircraft such as this little realised that the height of the Battle of France also marked the apogee of the Bf 110's career as a day-fighter.

Towards the end of the Battle of Britain, Fighter Command's basic combat formations began to change as a result of lessons learned earlier in the year. A clear example of this was the adoption of formations of three four-aircraft sections, instead of four three-aircraft Vics. In this photograph, taken in September 1940, No. 87 Sqn's 'A' Flight illustrates the new tactical formation, with Flt Lt Ian 'Widge' Gleed leading his charges on a patrol between Exeter and Bibury. This 'finger-four' formation was favoured by the *Jagdwaffe*, as it allowed each of the fighters to manoeuvre as required while still maintaining formation integrity. It also increased the pilots' field of view, thus improving each man's ability to scan the blind areas behind his section mates. Finally, greater awareness of the evolving combat situation meant that a pilot under attack could expect rapid support from his squadronmates.

as unflyable on the ground, and it would take Fighter Command until early July to make good these losses.

As mentioned, the first task given to the Luftwaffe in the early stages of the battle was the denial of the English Channel to British shipping in an offensive dubbed '*Kanalkampf*'. The Do 17s and Ju 87s charged with performing this mission would need fighter protection, and the long-range Bf 110 would be heavily involved in such operations, particularly over the southwest coast of England. As if a portent of things to come, the *Zerstörergruppen* lost nine aircraft in the first 72 hours of the offensive. Among those killed was Oberleutnant Hans-Joachim Göring, nephew of the Reichsmarschall. His 9./ZG 76 machine had been downed by Hurricane Is of No. 87 Sqn on 11 July, during an attack on Portland harbour.

As these losses clearly showed, the Bf 110 was not well suited to the role of close bomber escort. Units equipped with the aircraft had been trained to sweep ahead of

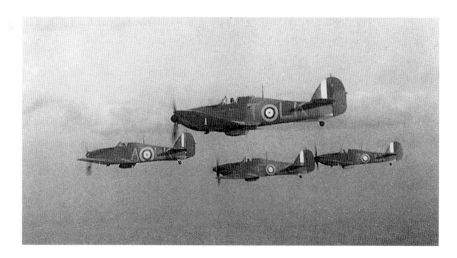

slow-flying bombers and clear the skies of enemy fighters through 'dive-and-zoom' attacks, using superior height, the element of surprise and the *Zerstörer*'s heavy armament to overwhelm their opponents. These advantages were lost when Bf 110s were 'shackled' to a formation of bombers, leaving fighter crews with little choice but to adopt their by-now-infamous defensive circles. The latter could also be used as a decoy manoeuvre for the bombers, as it filled a large area of sky with a prominent mass of wheeling aircraft. Such 'beehives' in turn attracted enemy fighters, so often served their major purpose.

One pilot who found circling Bf 110s irresistible was ace Flt Lt Adrian 'Ginger' Boyd of No. 145 Sqn, based at Tangmere. On 8 August his unit had been put on 'immediate readiness' to protect convoy CW9, codenamed *Peewit*, from attack by German bombers as it sailed in a westerly direction through the Straits of Dover. The convoy was targeted throughout the day, and No. 145 Sqn had five pilots killed as they attempted to defend the beleaguered vessels. The unit in turn claimed more than a dozen Ju 87s, Bf 109s and Bf 110s destroyed, no fewer than five of which were credited to Boyd. Two of his victories were *Zerstörer*, possibly from V.(Z)/LG 1. Forty-eight hours later he described this engagement in a BBC broadcast aimed at boosting civilian morale.

Unable to make contact with his squadronmates due to a faulty radio, Boyd had circled with his section of three Hurricane Is at 12,000ft directly overhead two large formations of Bf 110s that were wheeling around over the Channel 30 miles south of the Isle of Wight:

I was curious to know why they were circling round like that, and we decided to have a crack. We went down on them. The Messerschmitt which was at the end of the circling line of fighters was shot down into the sea immediately. Well, we broke up the happy little circle quite effectively. All three of us got at least one, and I think we must have taken them by surprise. I was attacked by a Messerschmitt 110 which I suppose I had overlooked. I skidded round and climbed for him, but he broke away to the left. I was still turning, and at about 1,000ft I stalled. He was right in my gunsights. I just gave him a quick burst, he heeled over and went straight into the sea and broke up. He was really a sitting duck.

A few hours later, fellow ace Flt Lt Frank Carey of No. 43 Sqn – also based at Tangmere – almost fell victim to a Bf 110 whilst trying to defend *Peewit*. Separated from the rest of his flight, he was stalking a formation of Bf 109s at around 20,000ft when, just as he positioned himself for an attack, all hell broke loose:

A very large explosion nearly blew me upside down. A Me 110 had seen what was happening, and it had come down and was sitting about 30yd behind me, and its

The Hurricane I quickly proved itself capable of withstanding considerable battle damage once combat was joined over France, as this No. 17 Sqn aircraft, coded 'YB–S', clearly shows. The starboard wing trailing edge ribs have been exposed by enemy machine gun fire, while a cannon shell has blown apart a section of flap. Fortunately for the anonymous pilot, the starboard wing main fuel tank (located immediately in front of the area of battle damage) appears to have escaped unscathed. The panel covering the aircraft's radios and oxygen bottles is missing. However, there is no damage in the immediate vicinity, so it may have been removed by the groundcrew upon the Hurricane's return to its dispersal. Damage of this magnitude usually meant the aircraft had to be taken out of the frontline and sent to a dedicated repair facility.

explosive 20mm shots had blown up all the ammunition in my port wing, leaving a hole big enough for a man to crawl through.

Carey had fallen victim to a classic 'dive-and-zoom' attack from a Bf 110 freed from protecting dive-bombers sent to attack the convoy. Despite having been wounded in the arm, Carey pressed on with his mission, only to be jumped again:

This time they blew one elevator and the rudder off and the aircraft did a half 'bunt' before I collected my senses. Having only about three-quarters of an aircraft left to control, I thought discretion was the better part of valour and slowly brought the remains back to base.

Carey's aircraft was almost certainly one of 18 British fighters that the *Zerstörergruppen* were credited with having destroyed on 8 August. Yet despite these successes demonstrating that the Bf 110s were at their most effective when freed to hunt for British fighters, the *Zestörergeschwaders* would continue to operate in the close-escort role well into August, during which time the Bf 110 units became both depleted and demoralised. Things came to a head on 13 August during the delayed launch of *Adlertag*, when bad weather played havoc with the Luftwaffe's carefully planned assault. Recall orders were sent out, which only added to the confusion among units involved as some did not receive the message. For example, the Bf 110s of V.(Z)/LG 1, charged with clearing the way for KG 54's Ju 88s targeting Portland harbour, flew into a veritable hornets' nest of British fighters. The efforts of the *Zerstörergruppen* were all in vain, however, as the bombers had remained on their airfields west of Paris.

ABOVE

Flt Lt J. B. Nicolson of No. 249 Sqn was not an ace – his solitary kill was the Bf 110 he attacked on 16 August 1940, as detailed below – yet he became the only member of Fighter Command to be awarded Britain's highest military honour, the Victoria Cross (VC). Nicolson, commanding 'A' Flight, was one of three pilots from his unit to engage German raiders striking at Gosport. It was his first time in combat. Nicolson was bounced out of the sun by a *Staffel* of Bf 109Es just before engaging the enemy, and his Hurricane I was set alight. However, he stayed with his stricken fighter long enough to claim a Bf 110 destroyed. Nicolson suffered serious burns to his hands before bailing out. He was awarded the VC for his bravery in November 1940. He is pictured here playing a Jew's harp while convalescing.

ENGAGING THE ENEMY

Like the Spitfire I/II, the Hurricane I was fitted with a Barr & Stroud GM 2 reflector gunsight as standard. This unit, devised by the Barr & Stroud company in 1935, featured a lens through which a large circular graticule was projected onto a circular glass reflector screen 76mm in diameter. The graticule was bisected by a cross, the horizontal bar of which was broken in the centre, with the range/base setting being determined using two knurled rings with their own scale that turned a perspex pointer to various range settings, and an adjustable ring which turned an indicator to indicate wingspan in feet. The internal mechanism then set the gap according to the required range. A central dot was added as a further aiming point.

The pilot first set the span dial to the known wingspan of his prospective target, then the range dial to the maximum for accurate fire. When the target coincided with the gap it was within range. The radius of the graticule ring gave the deflection allowance for hitting a target crossing at 100mph. The gunsight was illuminated by a half-silvered 12-volt lamp in a quick-release holder at the base of the sight body.

A substantial rubber pad was fitted to protect the pilot from injury in the event of a rough landing. Chosen by the RAF as its standard fixed gunsight, the GM 2 was known as the Reflector Sight Mk II in frontline service. The sight was patented in 1937, and the first examples of an initial order of 1,600 reached service squadrons in 1938. The GM 2 sight was used in most British fighters serving with both the RAF and the Fleet Air Arm between 1938 and 1943.

Five Bf 110s were shot down and three more damaged so badly that they had to be written off, prompting Reichmarschall Göring to furiously criticise his senior commanders in the field for allowing such a serious tactical blunder to take place:

The incident of V./LG 1 on 13 August shows that certain unit commanders have not yet learnt the importance of clear orders. I have repeatedly given orders that twin-engined fighters are only to be employed where the range of other fighters is inadequate, or where it is for the purpose of assisting our single-engined aircraft to break off combat. Our stocks of twin-engined fighters are not great, and we must use them as economically as possible.

OPPOSITE
Bf 110C 'A2+AL' of 6./ZG 2, pictured at Guyancourt, provides the backdrop for a meeting of the *Staffel*'s aircrew as they pore over details of the next mission.

Many *Zerstörer* were brought down over England, while others were so badly damaged that they did not make it back across the Channel. Few had their demise captured so graphically on film as this aircraft. It is apparently coded 'Yellow G', but references differ as to its exact identity. One source states that this dramatic telephoto sequence, shot from the French side of the Channel, shows the final moments of a 6./ZG 76 machine piloted by Feldwebel Jakob Birndorfer. If this is the case, the incident must have occurred early in the Battle of Britain and the crew must have been rescued, for Birndorfer was killed on 15 August 1940, trying to crash-land on the Isle of Wight. Another source suggests the Bf 110 may have been Wk-Nr. 3263 of III./ZG 26, shot down into the Channel on 25 September. Again, the crew (pictured in the water in the final photograph) was rescued unhurt by the *Seenotdienst*.

Two Bf 110s were also lost by 1./ZG 2 on 13 August during a late-afternoon mission escorting Ju 88s of III./LG 1 bound for Andover. Leutnant Wolfgang Münchmeyer was one of the pilots shot down:

The bombers were diving and disappearing in the clouds to seek their targets. So, we were free to look for possible adversaries, and by chance we found them in the form of Hurricanes flying at a lower altitude. I was flying as rearguard of our formation, and as we dived on them with increasing speed I was hit from below. I received two gunshots in my right foot from beneath and another one must have set the elevator steering out of control. Unable to clear the situation, we had to bail out. Bailing out, I hit the elevators of my aeroplane with my legs and landed with both legs fractured, suspended by my parachute in a tree.

Even heavier losses followed on 15, 16 and 18 August, when a total of 51 Bf 110C/Ds were destroyed in action or damaged beyond repair. Sixty Hurricane Is were also downed during the same period, but crucially only 21 pilots perished. By contrast, 87 *Zerstörer* crews had either been killed, posted missing or captured. These losses had a lasting effect on the *Zestörergeschwaders* for the rest of the Battle of Britain, as they were now struggling with both a shortage of aircraft and, more crucially, personnel to fly them. Göring, during a conference held at his Karinhall residence on 19 August, reiterated his view on how the remaining Bf 110s had to be used:

Twin-engined fighters are to be employed where the range of single-engined aircraft is insufficient, or where they can facilitate the breaking-off from combat of single-engined formations. The protection of returning bombers and fighters over the Channel must be assured by specially designated fighter formations.

In effect, Göring was ordering his *Zerstörer* crews even deeper into the lion's den in support of the hard-pressed *Kampfgeschwaders* as they attempted to bomb the RAF into

For a short time Hurricane I R4224 was the mount of No. 17 Sqn's newly arrived CO, Sqn Ldr A. G. Miller. He was forced to crash-land the aircraft near North Weald on 3 September 1940 after being attacked by a Bf 110 flown by Leutnant Kurt Sidow of 9./ZG 26.

submission. Certainly, Fighter Command was feeling the pressure from endless raids on its airfields and mounting losses in the air, but it was still capable of engaging the bomber formations and their escorts as they attacked targets primarily in Nos. 10 and 11 Group areas. Thanks to the reduction in their numbers, Bf 110 losses (28 aircraft in total) were bearable for the rest of August. However, the first week of September proved disastrous for the *Zerstörergeschwaders*, as no fewer than 48 Bf 110s were lost, with 17 of them destroyed on 4 September alone – and overall Luftwaffe losses that day were 28 aircraft destroyed. Among the Hurricane I pilots to engage the Bf 110s on 4 September was ace Plt Off Don Stones of No. 79 Sqn, based at Biggin Hill:

On 4 September we succumbed to temptation and went after 15 Me 110s which formed a defensive circle over Beachy Head. We attacked them, hoping to break up their circle, and got one of them in our first attack. I was so close to him before breaking away that I could see a red dragon painted on his nose. Fortunately for me, my squadronmate John Parker shot another 110 off my tail while I was dealing with the Red Dragon.

The 'Sharksmouths,' four leading *Experten,* all future Knight's Cross holders, pose for a photograph during the latter stages of the Battle of Britain. They are, from left: Oberleutnant Hans-Joachim Jabs and Oberleutnant Wilhelm Herget (both of 6./ZG 76), Hauptmann Erich Groth (*Gruppenkommandeur* of II./ZG 76) and Hauptmann Heinz Nacke (*Staffelkapitän* of 6./ZG 76).

The embattled *Zerstörergeschwaders* could not sustain the rate of losses suffered in the first week of September. Indeed, by now certain units were struggling to get enough serviceable aircraft and scratch crews to man them for the next wave of sorties. Yet somehow they struggled on, performing valuable escort duty for bomber formations tasked with striking key industrial targets in southwest England. One such mission was flown on 25 September, when 50 Bf 110s from ZG 26 covered 64 He 111s of KG 55 sent to attack the

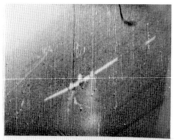

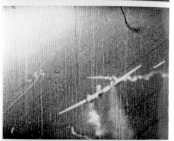

Bristol aviation works at Filton. Despite the mauling they had received at the hands of Fighter Command over the previous two-and-half months, the *Zerstörer* were still highly rated as escorts by *Kampflieger* such as gunner Robert Götz, serving with I./KG 55:

We are to attack an aircraft factory at Filton, and three Me 110 fighter groups have been announced as heavy fighter protection. Over Cherbourg, they in fact suddenly appear above us. It is a very reassuring feeling to see so many big two-engined fighters up there, with their shark's teeth and similar symbols painted on them. And these can accompany us much further inland than the single-engined Me 109, and are supposed to have terrifying firepower. But there have been rumours that they are by no means all that fast, as the circumstances would urgently require. However that may be, there they were as guardian angels, and they would soon show their teeth.

Three Bf 110s from ZG 26 and four He 111s were lost during the Filton mission. Given the scale of the RAF's reaction to this raid, the *Zerstörer* crews had done their job well. Two days later, in what would prove to be the last large-scale encounter between the Bf 110 and the Hurricane over England, the *Zerstörergeschwaders* endured their worst losses of the Battle of Britain when a staggering 19 aircraft (a number of them fighter-bombers) were downed as they attempted to attack industrial targets south of London. Hurricane I pilots alone claimed 39 Bf 110s destroyed on this date. One of these was credited to Plt Off Tom Neil of No. 249 Sqn, who paid tribute to the bravery of the rear gunner of one of the *Zerstörer* he attacked:

As I sought to drop into line astern 400yd behind the steeply turning 110, the rear-gunner fired, his tracer flicking past above and to the right of my head. I fired in response, which seemed to galvanise the aircraft in front into turning even more violently, causing – I was relieved to note – the gunfire from the rear to cease. The result of 'G' forces on the gunner, I though grimly, in which case keep the blighter turning! I fired again, this time from much closer range. The 110 dropped its nose and began to level out. Immediately, more fire from the rear cockpit, twisting and flicking in my direction so close that I flinched, expecting the metallic thud of bullets. Wow! Even closer now, less than 50yd and fear erased by surging adrenaline. The gunner ignored – forgotten. I fired again, tracer, sparks and twinkling flashes everywhere. The rear gunner responded with another burst that whipped into my face and over my head. A brave chap, by George! Would I be doing that in his position? I had a mental picture of the man sheltering behind the piece of armour plate, then jumping up and firing whenever the opportunity presented itself.

More Bf 110 losses occurred in early October, with seven aircraft from III./ZG 26 downed on 7 October while escorting a raid on the Westland aircraft works in Yeovil. However, as the scale of Luftwaffe operations reduced significantly, so did *Zerstörer*

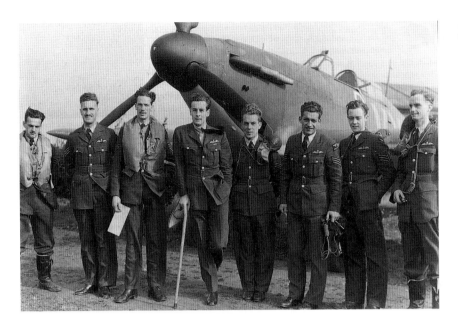

Ace pilot Sqn Ldr Peter Townsend is pictured leaning heavily on his walking stick at Church Fenton in mid-September 1940. He was suffering from a foot wound inflicted by a Bf 110 over Tunbridge Wells on 31 August. He is flanked by No. 85 Sqn's sergeant pilots. Townsend would claim a solitary Bf 110 on 18 August.

OPPOSITE
A Bf 110 is despatched by a Hurricane I over the Channel during the Battle of Britain. The 'kill' was recorded by the fighter's gun-camera, which operated automatically whenever the pilot fired his weapons. In the first frame the Bf 110 can be seen trying to escape by increasing speed – both DB 601s are at full throttle, as they are leaving trails of exhaust smoke in their wake. Tracer rounds from the Hurricane can be seen streaming through the air in the second and third frames, with an eventual hit on the port engine, which bursts into flames in the fourth frame.

activity recede. The requirement for daily close-escort missions for large daylight bomber formations fighting their way to and from the target was over. Fighter Command, and in particular the Hurricane I, had prevailed in the defence of Britain. The wholesale slaughter of the Bf 110 led to the dismemberment of the *Zerstörerwaffe* by the end of 1940. Perhaps the final word on the fate of the bomber-destroyer should go to eminent Luftwaffe historian and prolific Osprey author John Weal, who states in *Messerschmitt Bf 110 Zerstörer Aces of World War II*:

In a year of hard campaigning the Bf 110 had surpassed all expectations in Poland, excelled itself over the German Bight and Norway, fulfilled its role in France and been fought almost to extinction over England. Numbers never tell the whole story, but one Battle of Britain statistic is as stark as it is sobering. The Luftwaffe had embarked upon the Battle in July 1940 with 237 serviceable Bf 110 *Zerstörer*... and lost no fewer than 223 in the waging of it.

One of the 15 Bf 110s lost by ZG 26 on 18 August 1940 – the 'Hardest Day' – was Leutnant Hans-Joachim Kästner's '3U+EP', which crash-landed near Newchurch, Kent, after being damaged by a Hurricane I from No. 56 Sqn.

STATISTICS AND ANALYSIS

Bf 110s and Hurricane Is fought each other from 26 March 1940, when No. 73 Sqn engaged aircraft from 13./LG 1 over the Franco-German border, to 17 November 1940, when No. 17 Sqn claimed four Bf 110Cs from I./Erpr. Gr. 210 destroyed off Harwich. In the early months of 1941 the two types would only very occasionally engage each other in mortal combat, as virtually all *Zerstörergeschwaders* had been transferred away from the Channel front.

The Hurricane Is in France had enjoyed great success against the Bf 110s when the latter attempted to defend the *Kampf-* and *Stukageschwader* bombing targets during the *Blitzkrieg* in the West. As mentioned, the types fought each other on a near-daily basis from 10 May through to the start of the Dunkirk evacuation (Operation *Dynamo*) on 26 May. Once *Dynamo* had got under way, both France-based Hurricane I units and squadrons from Fighter Command's No. 11 Group combined to take the fight to the Luftwaffe, as the latter tried to interfere with the evacuation.

It was at this time that the Spitfire and the Bf 110 first encountered each other, and *Zerstörer* crews, like their single-seat brethren flying the Bf 109E, seemed to suffer severely from an 'affliction' dubbed 'Spitfire snobbery' by Hurricane units in 1940, both with respect to shooting them down and falling victim to them.

By the time *Dynamo* was completed at midnight on 2–3 June, the *Zerstörergruppen* had lost more than 60 Bf 110s in combat since 10 May. Of course, not all had fallen to Hurricane Is, but it would be fair to say that the major proportion had indeed been claimed by RAF fighter units. Some 87 Bf 110s were credited to Hurricane I pilots as destroyed between 10 May and the start of *Dynamo*; a further 32 were claimed between 26 May and 22 June.

Four of the six No. 601 Sqn pilots seen in this photograph (taken at a damp Exeter airfield in late September 1940) had 'made ace' by the end of the Battle of Britain, with a handful of Bf 110 kills included in their tallies. Flt Lt W. P. 'Billy' Clyde (second from left) scored nine and one shared destroyed, two probables and one and one shared damaged; Flg Off Tom Grier (sitting on the tailplane) claimed eight and four shared destroyed, one and one shared probable and one damaged (he was killed in action leading No. 32 Sqn over France on 5 December 1941; Flt Lt Sir Archibald Hope (wearing the Irvin jacket) was credited with one and one shared destroyed, two unconfirmed destroyed, three and one shared probable, four damaged, plus one or two more for which there are no details; and to Hope's left, Flt Lt H. C. Mayers, who had scored 11 and one shared destroyed, three and one shared probables and six damaged by the time he was lost in action leading No. 239 Wing in North Africa on 20 July 1942. Note No. 601 Sqn's 'winged-sword' emblem on the fin flash of this Hurricane.

Ten Hurricane I pilots were credited with five or more Bf 110s destroyed in 1940, and the two leading aces in this list (Flg Offs John Kilmartin and Leslie Clisby) claimed the bulk of their victories in France with No. 1 Sqn. Indeed, such was the ferocity of the initial clashes between this unit and the *Zerstörergruppen* in the wake of the German invasion that these men had claimed 12.5 victories between them by 17 May. However, by the latter date Clisby had been killed: he died on 14 May in combat against an overwhelming number of Bf 110s. The Australian was the only *Zerstörer* ace to lose his life to a bomber-destroyer in 1940.

Despite these successes, the experience of the Hurricane I squadrons in France actually demonstrated how not to fight an air war. The aircraft had been sent aloft in sections of three or flights of six each to face vastly superior numbers of enemy machines. To make matters worse, the tactical formations used were totally unsuited to engaging enemy fighters. In fact, the training of pilots to fly in tight formations had been given priority over gunnery and tactical instruction. As a result, a significant number of downed RAF pilots never saw the aircraft that bounced them.

Hurricane Is in France fought most of their engagements against bombers, reconnaissance aircraft or Bf 110s. And most of the Hurricane I's larger-scale combats, as well as losses, involved Bf 110s. Although the Hawker fighter proved more than able to handle the *Zerstörer* in individual combat (that is, dogfighting), Hurricane I sections and flights often found themselves overwhelmed by sheer weight of numbers. Bf 110 crews claimed exactly 30 Hurricane Is destroyed in France in May–June 1940, as well as a similar number of Spitfires mostly during *Dynamo*, although some of the latter were almost certainly misidentified Hurricane Is. Top Bf 110 *Zerstörer* aces Oberleutnant Hans-

The highest-scoring *Zerstörer Staffel* in terms of Hurricane Is claimed destroyed in 1940 was 6./ZG 76; two of its pilots claimed five successes. The *Staffelkapitän*, Hauptmann Heinz Nacke, was one of them. A veteran of the war in Spain, where he had flown long-range reconnaissance missions, Nacke would subsequently serve as *Kommandeur* of III./NJG 2, II./ZG 1 and ZG 101 through to war's end.

Leading Bf 110 Hurricane I Killers, 1940

Ace	Hurricane Kills	Final Score	Units(s) In 1940
Oblt Hans-Joachim Jabs	5	50	6./ZG 76
Hptm Heinz Nacke	5	14	6./ZG 76
Oblt Walter Borchers	4+	59	4./ZG 76
Hptm Eric Groth	4+	13	II./ZG 76
Oblt Theodor Rossiwall	4+	19	5./ZG 26
Oblt Sophus Baagoe	3+	14	8./ZG 26
Fw Helmut Haugk	3+	18	7./ZG 26
Uffz Richard Heller	3+	22	9./ZG 26
Oblt Wilhelm Herget	3+	72	6./ZG 76
Obstlt Johann Schalk	3+	15	III./ZG 26
Uffz Walter Scherer	3+	10	8./ZG 26
Ltn Botho Sommer	3+	7	III./ZG 26
Ltn Eduard Tratt	3+	38	1./ZG 1 and Erpr. Gr. 210
Ofhr Alfred Wehmeyer	3+	18	8./ZG 26

Oberleutnant Walter Borchers also enjoyed some success in 1940, being credited with four Hurricane Is destroyed (one during the Battle of France and three in the Battle of Britain) while serving as *Staffelkapitän* of 5./ZG 76. *Kommandeur* of III./NJG 5 in 1943 and *Kommodore* of NJG 5 in 1944, he had taken his score to 59 victories (12 during day missions in the Zerstörer) by the time he was killed in action on 5 March 1945.

Leading Hurricane I Bf 110 Killers, 1940

Ace	Bf 110 Kills	Final Score	Units(s) In 1940
Flg Off John Kilmartin	7	13 (+ 2 sh)	Nos. 1 and 43 Sqns
Flg Off Leslie Clisby	6.5	16 (+ 1 sh)	No. 1 Sqn
Flg Off William Clyde	6	9 (+ 1 sh)	No. 601 Sqn
Flg Off Ian Gleed	6	13 (+ 3sh)	No. 87 Sqn
Sgt Reginald Llewellyn	6	13 (+ 1 sh)	No. 213 Sqn
Plt Off Willie McKnight	6	17 (+ 2 sh)	No. 242 Sqn
Flg Off Manfred Czernin	5.5	13 (+ 5 sh)	No. 17 Sqn
Flt Lt Adrian Boyd	5	15 (+ 3 sh)	No. 145 Sqn
Flg Off Mark Brown	5	15 (+ 4 sh)	No. 1 Sqn
Flg Off Carl Davis	5	9 (+ 1 sh)	No. 601 Sqn

Joachin Jabs and Hauptmann Heinz Nacke claimed mainly French MS.406 fighters during the Battle of France, although Nacke also claimed two Spitfires over Dunkirk.

In the Battle of Britain a number of Hurricane I pilots claimed multiple Bf 110 victories either in an individual mission or during two or three sorties on the same day. These successes reflected the sheer number of *Zerstörer* present in the skies over southern England, particularly in the early phases of the battle, and their inability to defend themselves when tasked with close escort for bomber formations. Amongst the leading Hurricane I aces listed opposite, Flg Offs William 'Billy' Clyde and Carl Davis of No. 601 Sqn both claimed three Bf 110s on the south coast during the *Adlertag* massacre of 13 August. Two days later, Sgt Reg Llewellyn of No. 213 Sqn also got three off Portland Bill. Several of the remaining pilots on the list claimed pairs of Bf 110s in a single mission.

Between 9 July and 17 November 1940, Hurricane I pilots claimed 297 Bf 110s shot down. Actual *Zerstörer* combat losses during this period totalled 236 aircraft to all causes (mainly being shot down by Hurricane Is and Spitfires). In contrast, just 69 Hurricane I victories were credited to *Zerstörer* pilots during the same timeframe. Many Spitfire victories were also claimed, and again a percentage of these were probably in reality Hurricane Is. Jabs and Nacke claimed their Hurricane I kills in multiples, just as their RAF counterparts were doing, with Nacke claiming two on 15 August and three on the 30 August, and Jabs getting two on 1 September. Both pilots were then serving with 6./ZG 76 and both came through the Battle of Britain with Knight's Crosses.

At unit level, certain Hurricane I squadrons inflicted a heavy toll on the *Zerstörergeschwaders*, with No. 1 Sqn leading the way in the Battle of France by claiming 36 Bf 110s destroyed. No fewer than 14 of these were claimed on 11 May alone; actual losses amounted to six *Zerstörer*, to all causes. Similar overoptimistic claiming was a feature of the Battle of Britain too. For example, on 12 August No. 213 Sqn claimed 11 Bf 110s destroyed off the south coast, followed by 14 off Portland Bill three days later, while No. 87 Sqn claimed nine *Zerstörer* in the same action. Actual losses on this mission totalled 16 Bf 110s, some being downed by Spitfires from Nos. 234 and 609 Sqns.

Some overclaiming occurred within the *Jagdwaffe* too, but it did not go as far as within Fighter Command. Indeed, Bf 110 crews occasionally underclaimed – as on 18 May, when I./ZG 26 and II./ZG 76 were credited with six Hurricane Is destroyed when in fact 11 aircraft from seven different squadrons had been downed by the *Zerstörergeschwaders*. On 27 May, 8./ZG 26 downed six Hurricane Is from No. 145 Sqn near Dunkirk, all of which match Fighter Command figures, but the German unit then claimed seven on 14 June when in fact only a single aircraft from No. 242 Sqn was lost. During the epic clash off Portland on 15 August, V.(Z)/LG 1 and II./ZG 76 claimed 17 Hurricane Is between them but in fact only four were lost. The *Jagdwaffe's* II./ZG 76 was again in the thick of the action on 30 August when its pilots (including aces Nacke with three, Groth and Herget with two and Jabs and Borchers with one apiece) claimed 11 Hurricane Is destroyed. Very few of these match RAF losses, however. Few large-scale claims were made by the *Zerstörergeschwaders* after this date but Hurricane I squadrons, reinforcing their growing dominance in the skies over southern England, continued to make significant claims for Bf 110s into early October 1940. After that, the number of airworthy *Zerstörer* in France tailed off dramatically.

Flt Lt Ian 'Widge' Gleed and 'Figaro' (P2798) – named after the character from Walt Disney's film *Pinocchio* – pose for the camera soon after Gleed's arrival as replacement commander for No. 87 Sqn's 'A' Flight at Lille/Seclin on 17 May 1940. Future ace Plt Off R. P. 'Bee' Beamont had the following to say about Gleed's impact on the battle-weary unit: 'Gleed was one of our replacement pilots and he came out from the UK to tell us exactly how to run the war – all 5ft 6ins. of him! He was immediately as good as his word and tore into the enemy on every conceivable occasion with apparent delight and an entire lack of concern. His spirit was exactly what was needed to bolster up the somewhat stunned survivors of the week following May 10.'

AFTERMATH

Having suffered horrendous losses to Fighter Command during the Battle of Britain, the *Zerstörerwaffe* would never again be in a position to challenge the RAF in the skies over southern England. Clearly unable to hold its own against determined single-engined fighter attack, except under only the most advantageous of circumstance, the Bf 110 needed new employment. Three *Gruppen* were duly tasked with coastal patrol and convoy escort in the German Bight, off Norway and in the Mediterranean. Other aircraft and crews were transferred to the fledgling *Nachtjagd*, which had begun to receive a trickle of Bf 110s at the end of 1939. By VE-Day, the various *Nachtjagdgeschwaders* would have flown hundreds of Bf 110s and shot down countless heavy bombers as they attempted to defend German cities from attack by RAF Bomber Command.

The Hurricane too would remain a key RAF type until 1945, although after 1940 its role in Fighter Command began to steadily diminish as more and more units made the switch to the Spitfire. This meant clashes between the Hurricane (now predominantly in Mk II form) and the Bf 110 during daylight hours over western

Bf 110Ds' 'LT' and 'MT' of 9./ZG 26 go about their daily chores, patrolling Mediterranean airspace in 1941. Both machines are sporting 9. *Staffel's* 'cockerel' badge, while the former is also wearing the 'ladybird-in-a-diamond' emblem of III. *Gruppe*. The small white 'N' on the nacelle of the nearest aircraft indicates that it is powered by DB 601N engines.

Europe were a rare event. However, this was not the case in the eastern Mediterranean in the spring of 1941, as I. and II. ZG 26 supported the Wehrmacht's advance through the Balkans. In a situation not too far removed from the Battle of France one year earlier, a small number of Hurricane Is from the RAF's Nos. 33 and 80 Sqns fought valiantly in the face of overwhelming odds as they

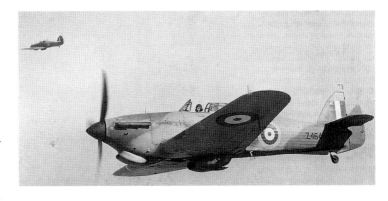

attempted to defend Greece. Bf 110 aces Hauptmann Theodor Rossiwall and Oberleutnant Sophus Baagoe claimed victories during the campaign, and in an action involving both men on 20 April the RAF's ranking ace of World War II, Sqn Ldr Marmaduke 'Pat' Pattle of No. 33 Sqn, was killed when his Hurricane was downed by a *Zerstörer* over Eleusis Bay.

By then III./ZG 26 had seen plenty of action supporting the *Afrika Korps* in the North African campaign. Flying from bases in Libya and Sicily, the unit carried out convoy patrols, anti-shipping strikes, bomber escort and *freie Jagd* missions from February 1941. Heavily involved in the fighting for Tobruk, the unit's crews routinely clashed with Hurricane Is from Nos. 73 and 274 Sqns, as well No. 3 Sqn Royal Australian Air Force. For example, on 3 April Flg Off Peter Turnbull from the latter unit was credited with four Bf 110s destroyed when the Hurricane Is bounced a formation of Ju 87s escorted by 7./ZG 26.

Bf 110s would continue to support the *Afrika Korps* in North Africa until the latter finally fled Tunisia in May 1943. From mid-1941 onwards, III./ZG 26 had operated more frequently as a ground attack unit, leaving much of the fighter work to *Jagdgruppen* equipped with Bf 109s that were now in-theatre. However, Bf 110s continued to clash with Hurricane IIs in North Africa well into 1942.

As with virtually all other frontline Luftwaffe types, the Bf 110 was heavily involved in supporting the invasion of the Soviet Union from June 1941. Here, its long range and heavy-hitting firepower proved great assets, as the *Zerstörergeschwaders* enjoyed a return to the glory days over Poland and France. Many victories were credited to Bf 110 pilots, including a number of ex-RAF Hurricanes supplied to the USSR from September 1941. Indeed, Feldwebel Theo Weissenberger of 1.(Z)/JG 77, flying in the far north, claimed eight Hurricanes destroyed as part of his tally of 23 victories in the Bf 110.

It is almost certainly the case that the last time the Hurricane and Bf 110 clashed in World War II was over the frozen north of the USSR in early 1943. By then no longer considered suitable for the day-fighter role for which they had originally been designed, both types nevertheless soldiered on through to war's end fulfilling other missions such as nightfighting and ground attack.

BIBLIOGRAPHY

BOOKS

Bungay, Stephen, *The Most Dangerous Enemy* (Aurum, 2000)

Cornwall, Peter D., *The Battle of France Then and Now* (After the Battle, 2007)

Cull, Brian, Bruce Lander with Heinrich Weiss, *Twelve Days in May* (Grub Street, 1995)

Dick, AVM Ron, *Hurricane: RAF Fighter* (Airlife, 2000)

Drake, Billy, with Christopher Shores, *Billy Drake: Fighter Leader* (Grub Street, 2002)

Foreman, John, *Battle of Britain: The Forgotten Months* (Air Research Publications, 1988)

Foreman, John, *1941: The Turning Point. Part 1: The Battle of Britain to the Blitz* (Air Research Publications, 1993)

Foreman, John, *RAF Fighter Command Victory Claims of World War Two. Part 1: 1939–1940* (Red Kite, 2003)

Franks, Norman, *RAF Fighter Command Losses of the Second World War* (Midland Publishing, 1997)

Franks, Norman, *Air Battle Dunkirk* (Grub Street, 2000)

Franks, Richard A., *The Hawker Hurricane: A Comprehensive Guide for the Modeller* (*Modeller's Datafile 2*) (SAM Publications, 1999)

Green, William, *Warplanes of the Third Reich* (Doubleday, 1972)

Holmes, Tony, *Hurricane Aces 1939–40* (*Osprey Aircraft of the Aces 18*) (Osprey, 1998)

Jefford, C. G., *RAF Squadrons* (Airlife, 2001)

Kent, Gp Capt J. A., *One of the Few* (Corgi, 1975)

Ketley, Barry and Mark Rolfe, *Luftwaffe Fledglings 1935–1945* (Hikoki Publications, 1996)

Lake, Jon, *The Battle of Britain* (Silverdale Books, 2000)

Neil, Wg Cdr Tom, *Gun Button to 'Fire'* (William Kinber, 1987)

Obermaier, Ernst, *Die Ritterkreuzträger der Luftwaffe Jagdflieger 1939–1945* (Dieter Hoffmann, 1966)

Price, Dr Alfred, *World War II Fighter Conflict* (Purnell, 1975)

Ramsey, Winston (ed.), *The Battle of Britain Then and Now, Mk IV* (After the Battle, 1987)

Richey, Wg Cdr Paul, *Fighter Pilot* (Jane's, 1980)

Shores, Christopher, *Aces High: Volume 2* (Grub Street, 1999)

Shores, Christopher and Clive Williams, *Aces High* (Grub Street, 1994)

Stedman, Robert F., *Jagdflieger: Luftwaffe Fighter Pilot 1939–45* (*Osprey Warrior 122*) (Osprey 2008)

Stones, Donald, *Dimsie* (Wingham Press, 1991)

Sturtivant, Ray, *The History of Britain's Military Training Aircraft* (Haynes, 1987)

Thomas, Andrew, *Hurricane Aces 1941–45* (*Osprey Aircraft of the Aces 57*) (Osprey, 2003)

Townsend, Peter, *Duel of Eagles* (Weidenfeld, 1990)

Van Ishoven, Armand, *Messerschmitt Bf 110 at War* (Ian Allan, 1985)

Vasco, John J., *Luftwaffe Colours: Zerstörer. Vol. 1: Luftwaffe Fighter-Bombers and Destroyers, 1936–1940* (Classic Publications, 2005)

Vasco, John J. and Peter D. Cornwall, *Zerstörer: The Messerschmitt 110 and its Units in 1940* (JAC Publications, 1995)

Vasco, John J. and Fernando Estanislau, *Messerschmitt Bf 110C, D and E: An Illustrated Study* (Classic Publications, 2008)

Weal, John, *Messerschmitt Bf 110 Zerstörer Aces of World War II* (*Osprey Aircraft of the Aces 25*) (Osprey, 1999)

WEBSITES

Kacha, Petr 2007 *Aces of the Luftwaffe*. Available online at: <www.luftwaffe.cz>

Wood, Tony 2010 *Combat Claims and Casualties*. Available online at: <www.lesbutler.ip3.co.uk/tony/tonywood.htm>

INDEX